All About
Heaven

What the Bible Tells Us

Randy Petersen

Publications International, Ltd.
Lincolnwood, IL 60712

Randy Petersen is the author of *Why Me, God?* and coauthor of *Jesus: His Life and Times.* He earned a B.A. in ancient languages from Wheaton College before becoming executive editor of *Bible Newsletter* and other publications. He has written more than 30 books, including *The Family Book of Bible Fun,* and has contributed to the *Revell Bible Dictionary* and the *Quest Study Bible.*

ISBN: 1-4127-1312-9

Manufactured in USA.

8 7 6 5 4 3 2 1

Contents

Heading to Our Heavenly Home

Heaven is up there, out there, somewhere beyond here. We vaguely hope to go there someday, but not especially soon. "Out of sight, out of mind," they say—and heaven is definitely out of sight. Probably because we can't see it, we don't think about it so much. It's the daily grind that grabs us. "Don't bother me with eternity; just let me get through today!"

What is heaven? What will it be like? Most people just shrug. They really don't know.

Well, God knows. And he has revealed a great deal about heaven in the pages of the Bible. The language is poetic and full of vivid pictures. The reality is that heaven is probably far beyond our comprehension. Still, the Bible gives us glimpses from the Old and

New Testament. From the words of Isaiah, Jesus, John, Paul, and others, we can piece together a sketch of that amazing place.

If you're taking a trip to some exotic location, you buy a guidebook or go online. You view pictures of the place and learn what the experts say about your destination. What will the accommodations be? How's the weather? What will you do for fun? How should you prepare for this trip?

Should it be any different when you're headed for heaven? The Bible makes a great guidebook for this trip, so let's see what these experts—the biblical writers—tell us about what to expect and how to prepare.

Lure, Longing, and Legends

Common Misinterpretations of Heaven

Some people think of heaven as an endless, boring church service. Others have the notion that we become angels when we die. Many assume that heaven is merely a state of mind. The Bible, however, teaches otherwise.

There is an old joke about a preacher who was going on and on about eternal life. "Who in this room wants to go to heaven?" he thundered. "Everyone who wants to go to heaven, stand up!" The whole congregation rose to their feet—except for one young boy in the front pew of the church. The preacher glowered down at him and said, "What about you, son? Don't you want to go to heaven when you die?"

"Oh, sure," the lad responded, "*when I die.* I thought you were getting a busload to go now."

Many of us are like that boy. Heaven is a distant promise for us, something we look forward to down the road, but it's an exit we're not quite ready to take yet. No matter how devout we are in our beliefs, death still scares us. And that's understandable since we don't know a whole lot about what lies beyond. Although the Bible gives us some snapshots, it's hard to piece them together into a panoramic view.

We are going to do just that, compiling the biblical images and doctrines, the metaphors and the hints, to get a fuller understanding of that future world.

Cloud-Sitting

According to a recent poll, 85 percent of Americans believe in the afterlife. The majority of us agree that physical death is not the end. But what's next? What kind of life follows our earthly existence? Some believe the soul gets reincarnated. Others say the soul lives on in some spiritual realm. But a full two-thirds of the U.S. population maintains that we go to heaven or hell when we die.

∽∽∽∽∽

According to a recent poll, 85 percent of Americans believe in the afterlife.

∽∽∽∽∽

Strangely enough, people seem to have a more vivid picture of hell than of heaven. They imagine fiery torment, not a place you'd want to visit. But what is heaven really like? That's where the picture gets fuzzy.

It's the preferred destination—no question about it—but why? What does heaven have to offer? Why would we want to move into that neighborhood and live there forever? Unfortunately, the common notions of heaven leave much to be desired.

For one thing, people expect heaven to be boring.

No doubt you've seen cartoons where people die and suddenly they're angels, sitting on clouds, flapping wings and strumming harps. The Bible does suggest that we'll be making music in heaven, but we certainly won't become angels. It's very clear that angels are separate beings, not former humans. (Jesus did mention that we would be "like" the angels in heaven, but he was undoubtedly referring to our common activity—that is, praising the Lord.)

But if you have that cloud-sitting picture in your head, it's understandable that heaven might seem dull to you. There are only so many stanzas of "Holy, Holy, Holy" you can strum before it gets stale. And of course were talking about eternity.

That's the problem, isn't it? Eternity. Even the best things in life lose their flavor when they go on too long. You may love watching baseball games, but by the 25th inning your interest would likely wane. Go to a concert of your favorite musician, and still, by the fifth encore you'd be checking your watch. We don't like the thought of anything going on forever. Certainly not a church service.

Some of our best glimpses of heaven come from Revelation, the last book of the Bible. The apostle John, who wrote this book, shares the wondrous and fascinating things he saw there: The twenty-four elders and the four living creatures fell down and worshiped God who is seated on the throne, saying, "Amen. Hallelujah!" And from the throne came a voice saying, "Praise our God, all you his servants, and all who fear him, small and great." Then I heard what seemed to be the voice of a great multitude, like the sound of many waters and like the sound of mighty thunder peals, crying out, "Hallelujah! For the Lord our God the Almighty reigns. Let us rejoice and exult and give him the glory" (Revelation 19:4–7).

You can tell that John was having a great time. Nevertheless, although this was a truly amazing display, it still sounds like a church service. And if people get bored with three songs and a twenty-minute sermon, you can't blame them for fearing the tedium of an eternal church meeting.

No Fun?

People often think of heaven in terms of what is not there. No sorrow, no suffering, and no sin. And didn't Jesus say something about no marriage? Lots of people jump to the conclusion that it will also be *no* fun.

Sure enough, we read in Revelation that "he will wipe every tear from their eyes. Death will be no more; mourning and crying and pain will be no more" (Revelation 21:4). That was a precious promise to first-century Christians who were going through persecution. John was probably penning

Continued on page 14

In Heaven Will People Be Married?

Shortly before his crucifixion, Jesus held a kind of press conference. But instead of reporters, lawyers and religious leaders tried to trip him up with their trick questions. One of these involved marriage and heaven.

Man marries woman. Man dies. According to Jewish law, the man's brother is responsible to marry the widow and raise the children as his own. So, the brother marries the woman, but he also dies. The next brother marries her, and he dies. At this point, you might be wondering what she's putting in the pot roast. But by the end of this hypothetical situation, seven brothers have married her, and they've all died. Then she dies.

"So, Jesus, in heaven whose wife will she be?"

Here's how Jesus responded: "You are wrong, because you know neither the scriptures nor the power of God. For in the resurrection they neither marry nor are given in marriage, but are like angels in heaven. And as for the resurrection of the dead, have you not read what was said to you by God, 'I am the God of Abraham, the God of Isaac, and the

God of Jacob'? He is God not of the dead, but of the living"(Matthew 22:29–32).

Does that mean that your marriage will not be valid in heaven? Will you have no connection to your beloved spouse? That idea troubles a lot of people, but let's look at what Jesus was actually saying.

First, remember that it was a trick question. The askers belonged to a sect that did not believe in heaven (or in angels). They were trying to make the notion of heaven seem absurd.

Second, consider the nature of marriage in ancient times. Sadly, in most cases little love was involved. Women had few rights, and marriage was often a matter of property transfer. The Jewish law in question was actually an attempt to ensure that widows and orphans would have some means of support.

That may give us a clue as to why Jesus talks about "marrying" and being "given in marriage" rather than the state of being in a marriage. He may not be saying that marriages will not exist in heaven, but that there will be no need for the kind of economic relationship he was being asked about.

Some have surmised that heaven will not need new marriages because it will not need new children. Others point out that marriage itself is a symbol of our relationship with Christ, and we won't need that symbol once we can experience the fullness of knowing Christ.

The key to Jesus' answer is "the power of God." The askers were nitpicking. They were thinking too small. Certainly the living God would have the power to solve this hypothetical problem. We can trust him to do so. And, from what we know of God, would he have any desire to do away with loving human relationships? No! Such relationships are a key part of his kingdom. All of this suggests that, while heaven would have no place for economic obligation, jealousy, and possessiveness, the loving relationship of a married couple might be preserved and even enhanced.

Continued from page 11

Revelation toward the end of the first century, during the time when Roman Emperor Domitian was demanding to be worshiped as "Lord and God." Of course, Christians couldn't comply, so they faced Rome's wrath—arrest, sometimes torture and death. In tough times like that, John's vision of heaven was seen as a paradise. No death, mourning, crying, or pain! Hallelujah!

∽∽∽

> *If you're not allowed to laugh in heaven, I don't want to go there.*
>
> Martin Luther

Nowadays, however, few of us suffer to that extent. In fact, some armchair philosophers suggest that we *need* a little suffering in our lives to make the good times feel better. For example, Chicago's White Sox fans might not have had such a thrill with their 2005 World Series win if they hadn't suffered frustration for nearly a century beforehand.

It's not suffering, however, that's the issue. It's the supposed lack of fun in heaven.

In Mark Twain's classic novel *Huckleberry Finn*, a Christian lady tells Huck about heaven and warns him that, in order to get there, he'll have to behave better. Huck then asks if his buddy Tom Sawyer will be there, and the lady says that such a bad boy certainly won't. "I was glad about that," says Huck, "because I wanted him and me to be together."

⛓⛓⛓

Let's dispose of that silly idea that it's better to party with the hot list in hell than to worship with the angels in heaven.

⛓⛓⛓

That's a pretty common notion among modern folks. They think about all the good Christians headed for heaven, and they think about all the "sinners" who aren't, and they ask, "Which party would I rather go to?" To some, sin seems like harmless fun, and righteousness seems boring. So maybe you'll dance in eternal flames, but at least you'll be partying with people who know how to have a good time.

Sadly, we Christians have earned that attitude. Too often our churches are places of judgment rather than joy, of anger rather than acceptance, of hubris rather than humility, of growling rather than grace. No wonder our neighbors don't want to spend eternity with us.

But this attitude also ignores the many dangers of sin. It's not harmless fun. Infidelity wrecks families. Drugs fry brains. Unbridled selfishness leads to violence and destruction. One view of hell is that God just removes himself from the scene and lets sin feed on itself. Sin becomes its own punishment.

So let's dispose of that silly idea that it's better to party with the hot list in hell than to worship with the angels in heaven. Hell is not a dance club for the benignly naughty. It's a cesspool of vicious appetite and unrelenting hunger. Heaven is not a home for the bland. Indeed, it's a whole different dimension.

Thank You, Einstein

*H*ave you studied physics lately? Probably not, but you should. If you're like me, in the years since you attended classes in school, it has changed. A lot.

Physics is the scientific study of the forces that affect our universe. Have those forces been changing? Of course not. But our understanding of those forces has changed immensely. (By "our understanding" I mean the views of those scientists who actually understand these things.)

Isaac Newton had it figured out. Or he thought he did. He said that every action has an equal and opposite reaction, that how things move through space over time can be measured, and that the force of gravity or electromagnetism can be determined. Master a few equations, and you've pretty much know how things work.

Then Einstein challenged that idea, with the help from lesser-known scientists. The twentieth century saw a total rethinking of physics. Newton's laws still worked within a closed system, but scientists were seeing how open the universe really was. Relativity became a buzzword. Everything changed—including space and time. In these new equations, space and time bent and folded over on themselves.

This is not a science textbook, so we won't delve into any more of those details. The point is, scientists began to think in a whole new dimension. If you were to enroll in a college physics course tomorrow, it might take you a month to move beyond your Newtonian assumptions and open your mind to Einsteinian possibilities.

***

We need to think in a new dimension. Most of the misconceptions of heaven are a result of small thinking.

***

The same is true when we think of heaven. We need to think in a new dimension. Most of the misconceptions of heaven are a result of small thinking. We think of heaven merely as the best of earth. On earth, ball games have winners and losers; winners rejoice and losers lament. But why couldn't the Architect of heaven invent games where everyone wins in different ways, where losers grow through a new challenge, and where the game itself unfolds into new joys every moment?

◦◦◦◦◦◦

*The most important thing about
heaven is that God is there.*

◦◦◦◦◦◦

If you are thinking in earthbound ways, your worries about boredom in heaven might make sense. But you're missing a crucial detail: God. The most important thing about heaven is that God is there. And everything you think you know about God now—well, Paul says we are just looking through a darkly tinted window (1 Corinthians 13:11). When we see him face to face, in all his fullness, we will be dazzled. He will take us to a completely different dimension.

Life, Love, and Truth

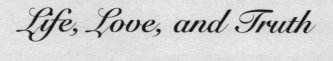

To get an idea of heaven's grandeur, there are many aspects of God's being we could consider, but let's choose three. God is life. God is love. And God is truth.

Boredom is a kind of death. Your interest dies. Your mental activity ceases. It's a shame that too many church services elicit that response. It really shouldn't be that way because God is the author of life. He raises us from the dead. His spirit breathes into our lives and awakens us from slumber.

In heaven we will encounter God in all his fullness. The power of life will be flowing through us, energizing us eternally. Think about a time when you felt most fully alive. Gazing at the Grand Canyon. Playing badminton with your kids. Singing Handel's *Messiah*. Whatever it was for you, you can be sure heaven will be all that and far more.

Now think about a time when you were most deeply in love. (Maybe that's right now!) Not puppy love, not shallow infatuation, but a deep sense of interest in another person and a feeling that the other person knows and accepts you, too. You could spend hours with that person, and it would seem like seconds. You could spend years in love with that person, and it would seem like a moment. And maybe you have.

Now multiply that feeling by ten, or a hundred, or a million. God is love, we are told in Scripture. His love for us has eternal dimensions. In Romans, Paul writes, "For I am convinced that neither death, nor life, nor angels, nor rulers, nor things present, nor things to come, nor powers, nor height, nor depth, nor anything else in all creation, will be able to separate us from the love of God in Christ Jesus our Lord" (Romans 8:38–39).

So you won't be spending eternity sitting on a cloud staring into space. You'll be gazing into the face of the One you love, the One who knows everything about you and still loves you more than anyone else does.

How well did you do in school? Some kids seem to have a thirst for knowledge that drives them to excel. Some of them go on into professions where they continue to learn more and more. Is that your story?

Or do you hunger for more unconventional knowledge? Many people today couldn't care less about algebra or physics, but they read everything they can find about movies, golf, or soap operas. What's your specialty? Are you a Civil War buff or a sci-fi nut? Do you memorize Bible verses, stock prices, or batting averages?

Will St. Peter Greet Us at the Pearly Gates?

You've heard a million jokes about this, but does it have any basis in Scripture? Yes, a little. In Matthew 16, after Peter expressed his faith in Jesus as the Messiah, Jesus highly commends the apostle. Jesus declares him (or his faith) as the "rock" on which the church will be built. He also says, "I will give you the keys of the kingdom of heaven" (Matthew 16:19).

This provided a snapshot of Peter as the "keeper of the keys," and it only made sense that he would hang around the entry gate of heaven in order to let people in or keep them out. That's a bit of legend that developed around that image. No other Scripture shows Peter in that role.

Several interpretations of those verses are in Matthew 16, as well as a major difference between Catholics and Protestants. In Catholic teaching, Jesus established Peter as the head of the Church (the first Pope) and that people would enter heaven only through the Church. Protestants tend to say

Peter's faith was the rock on which the church will be built and that anyone who shares the good news of Jesus (as Peter and those first disciples did) will unlock the gates of God's kingdom for those who believe.

As for the "pearly gates," that's a detail from Revelation 21, where an angel takes John on a tour of the heavenly city. The earthly Jerusalem had walls, with gates here and there to allow passage. These gates could be closed at night or in wartime, but generally they were just openings in the wall. In ancient times city gates became meeting places and markets, and so they were often built up and decorated more than the surrounding walls. John described the heavenly Jerusalem laid out as a perfect square, with walls that have twelve gates, three on each side. "Each of the gates is a single pearl" (Revelation 21:21). And it's interesting to note that these gates never close.

The point is that God made our brains to learn. As we go through life, we all learn *something*. Even the worst students have some subjects that interest them, whether or not those subjects are part of the official curriculum. We like to know new stuff.

That's another way that heaven will delight us. God is there, and God is truth. The Bible often mentions things that "surpass our understanding"— but in heaven we will have access to what God knows. You think the Internet is cool? Wait until you tap into the Lord's omniscience.

The Full Picture

Have you ever seen a breathtaking view and tried to take a photo? Say the sun is setting over the ocean, wisps of clouds are turning magenta and peach over the deep blue water. A sailboat leans and circles in the distance. Gulls are playing tag as foamy water laps up onto the shore. You see the silhouette of a couple strolling hand in hand along the beach. Get the picture?

*Every saint in heaven is as a
flower in the garden of God, and
every soul there is as a note in some
concert of delightful music.*

Jonathan Edwards

Well, no. You don't get the picture. No photograph could capture that stunning experience. You might catch a color or shape, but when you show the prints to your neighbors, you will end up saying, "You had to be there."

The Bible gives us glimpses of heaven, a photo album of sorts. "Look, there are the mansions. There are the pearly gates. There are the streets of gold. There is the dazzling brilliance of the Lord himself." But words cannot capture the fullness of that experience. We have to imagine what it must be like, and even our imagination falls short. You just have to be there.

And someday we will be.

Lord,

The idea of heaven thrills me but also scares me a little. There's so much I don't know about it. I do look forward to being with you forever. Help me trust you with the details.

In Jesus' name. Amen.

No Other Way to Talk About It

What Heaven Is Imagined to Be

Is heaven really a place, or is it just a state of mind? Are the pearly gates and streets of gold really there, or is that description merely poetic license? Will we have bodies in heaven or live just as spirits? Some folks think the intelligent way to think about heaven is to shake off all those poetic details. But shouldn't we trust the Bible to give us the best way to talk about this unfathomable reality?

When Jimmy's grandmother passed away, the boy's parents carefully explained that she was far, far away with God in heaven. Someday, they said, the whole family would see her again when they are in heaven, too. It was the true-but-simple story you give to a child, and these parents did well with it.

The next summer, the whole family planned a vacation to the West Coast from their midwestern home. They'd make a long drive, seeing sights along the way. In preparation, they told little Jimmy that they'd be spending lots of time in the car, and it would take several days. He would have to be very good and very patient because they were going far, far away, all the way to California.

The boy mulled it over, and then a thought struck him. "California? Is that next to heaven?"

Picture Language

It made sense to Jimmy. Heaven was a place far, far away, and so was California. Maybe they could take a side trip and see Grandma. We laugh at his simple thinking, but should we? California is a real place, but isn't heaven real, too? There are some transportation issues involved, and heaven

So If Heaven Is a Place, Where Is It?

It's got to be an island in the South Pacific, don't you think?

Seriously, we don't know. It's best not to think of it geographically. You're not going to stumble on it while hitchhiking to Tulsa. And no spacecraft will pass through heaven on its way through the galaxy. There's only one way to get to heaven, and that's by God's grace. In the same way, we don't know where God will place his New Heaven and New Earth.

With physics, it's possible to imagine alternate dimensions or parallel universes in which heaven might be situated. But don't overanalyze this question. God has told us about heaven to encourage us. Heaven is not a puzzle to solve. The directions remain quite simple: Turn around and yield to Jesus.

is impossible to map, but it is just as real as California, probably more so.

So are we really saying heaven is a physical place? Does it have the actual substance of, say, Cleveland or Asia or Neptune?

Well, yes and no, and yes.

The Bible speaks of heaven in physical terms. It's not some imaginary place. Scripture describes how heaven looks and feels, who will be there, and what goes on there. The language is vivid.

You may ask: Doesn't the Bible use poetic imagery to describe spiritual things? Sure. When the psalmist spoke of being comforted by the Lord's "rod and staff," is the psalmist saying that God actually reaches out with a shepherd's tools? No, it's a picture used to convey a relationship that goes beyond physical details.

With this in mind, some people try to cast aside all the vivid depictions of heaven as mere fancy. They tell us to forget about streets of gold and mansions and jeweled gates. That's just ancient poetry used to support the main point, which is heaven is a nice place where we all want to go. After death, if we're fortunate, our souls will inhabit this spiritual realm.

That seems to make a lot of sense, especially to modern-minded folks who don't want to sound too religious. The problem is, it misses the main point of biblical teaching about heaven and our resurrection from death. It allows us to make up our own minds about this spiritual afterworld, but it ignores the first-hand testimony from an actual resident.

⌒⌒⌒⌒⌒

Rather than trying to figure out what heaven should be, we ought to listen to the One who lives there.

⌒⌒⌒⌒⌒

Imagine a church gathering a task force to plan a new ministry in a nearby city. In their initial meeting they go on and on about their views of the city—who lives there, what life is like there, and what kind of help people need. Then one woman stands up in the back of the room. "It's been interesting to hear you talk about my city. But I live there, and it's pretty obvious that you don't. Would you like to hear my view of what life is like where I live?" Of course, they listen to her first-hand perspective, as they should.

Rather than trying to figure out what heaven should be, we ought to listen to the One who lives there. Jesus, who came from heaven and is there now, once chided a Pharisee for ignoring the truth. "If I have told you about earthly things and you do not believe, how can you believe if I tell you about heavenly things? No one has ascended into heaven except the one who descended from heaven, the Son of Man" (John 3:12–13).

So if you want to know about heaven, ask the experts. What did Jesus say about it? What has God revealed in Scripture? The language may be fanciful, or poetic, or seem exaggerated, but let's give God the benefit of the doubt. Maybe he has told us exactly what he wants us to know.

Otherwise Unspeakable

~~~

here's a wonderful phrase scholars use for the poetic language of Scripture. They acknowledge that the metaphors in the Bible are physical terms for realities that go far beyond the physical realm, but they say such realities are "otherwise unspeakable." That is, there's no better way to describe them.

Let's test this out. Think about streets of gold. See those thoroughfares in your mind's eye, gleaming, glittering, no matter how many feet tread upon them. Now consider the "common-sense" translation: "Heaven is a beautiful place for your soul after you die."

Will the streets actually be paved with the soft metallic element we denote with the chemical symbol "Au"? Maybe, maybe not. But we lose an awful lot in the translation to "beautiful place." When

The One remains, the many
change and pass;
Heaven's light forever shines,
Earth's shadows fly;
Life, like a dome of many-colored glass,
Stains the white radiance of Eternity.

Percy Shelley (Adonais 50, 2)

people make that translation, when they trade in the poetic images of Scripture for more literal descriptions, they're usually trying to sound more intelligent. But they're actually "dumbing down" the true message.

The only way for God to describe the brightness of his presence is to say that even the streets will shine like gold. That's something we can see and imagine. The full reality would not fit in our brains. So let's understand that the biblical descriptions are poetic images, but let's also accept them as God's way of talking about heaven. Rather than reducing these images to more "realistic" expressions, let's understand that the reality is certainly far more dazzling than we could ever know—and yet God asks us to envision it in these physical ways.

The Importance of Physicality

There's another issue under the surface, which may be a problem for you. Many people have the notion that physical things are less important than spiritual things. As we look to the future, we see a spiritual existence in heaven and assume that our physical bodies will be long gone. Surprisingly, the Bible doesn't teach that.

"God is spirit," the Bible says (John 4:24), and many thus assume that the eternal world is completely nonphysical. But we forget who said that. It was Jesus, who was God-in-the-flesh and who, by the way, stopped to have this conversation because he was thirsty. The Incarnation of Jesus is certainly one of the great mysteries of our faith, but it is the foundation of Christianity. Spirit and body came together in that God-man.

In both the Old and New Testaments, the Bible consistently teaches a unity of the spiritual life and the physical life. Yes, the apostle Paul often distinguished between Spirit and "flesh," but it's apparent from the context that he's talking about a physical life that follows the Spirit as opposed to a physical life that ignores the Spirit. It's true that physical impulses without the guiding force of God's Spirit lead to sin, death, and destruction. But the ideal is not a disembodied spiritual life; rather it's a physical life that is intimately connected with God's Spirit. Spirit and body together—that's what God wants.

And so the biblical pictures of God's ultimate redemption are unabashedly physical. God doesn't just take our souls to heaven; he creates a New Heaven and a New Earth (Revelation 21:1). He doesn't let our bodies rot away; he gives us new, imperishable bodies.

"Listen, I will tell you a mystery!" said Paul. "We will not all die, but we will all be changed, in a moment, in the twinkling of an eye, at the last trumpet. For the trumpet will sound, and the dead will be raised imperishable, and we will be changed. For this perishable body must put on imperishability, and this mortal body must put on immortality" (1 Corinthians 15:51–53).

It may make perfect sense to assume that we merely live on in some spiritual existence, or in a

◇◇◇◇◇◇

It may make perfect sense to assume that we merely live on in some spiritual existence, or in a "state of mind," after our bodies die, but that's not what the Bible teaches.

◇◇◇◇◇◇

"state of mind," after our bodies die, but that's not what the Bible teaches. In those sacred pages we find a God who loves the physical universe he has created. He loves it so much that he entered it, as a physical being, to redeem it, and he will remake it at the end of time. And let us not ever forget—he will also remake us.

Now and Then

When do we get that imperishable body? And what happens to us in the meantime? We find only two distinct transition events in Scripture and two kinds of heaven that may await us.

Our most vivid pictures of heaven come from the end of Revelation. This final book of the Bible actually describes the New Heaven and New Earth (and New Jerusalem) that God will create at the end of time. That is our eternal home.

The Bible pictures a series of events leading up to that re-creation. You have just read about the "last trumpet," which signals the Second Coming of Christ when Jesus returns to establish his kingdom on earth. You may also be familiar with terms like Rapture, Tribulation, Armageddon, and Millennium. There are several theories about the order of those end-time events, and we're not going to figure it all out here. The key is that, at some point in that process, we are "changed"—given our new resurrection bodies to reign with Christ and live with him forever.

But what happens if we die before all that happens? Where do we go then?

The Thessalonians were wondering the same thing. They were expecting the return of Christ at any moment, but some of their loved ones were dying. Would dead Christians be excluded from the Second Coming?

Not at all, said Paul. In fact, they'll get front-row seats. "For the Lord himself, with a cry of command,

Do People in Heaven See Us on Earth?

Yes, several cases in Scripture suggest they do. When Samuel came back to confer with King Saul, he was aware of recent things Saul had done (1 Samuel 28:16–19). At the Mount of Transfiguration, when Moses and Elijah met with Jesus, they seemed to be up to speed on events in his ministry (Luke 9:31).

with the archangel's call and with the sound of God's trumpet, will descend from heaven, and the dead in Christ will rise first. Then we who are alive, who are left, will be caught up in the clouds together with them to meet the Lord in the air; and so we will be with the Lord forever" (1 Thessalonians 4:16–17). Those who have died will "rise" to join this glorious, end-time event. Presumably, they will be given imperishable bodies, too.

So what happens if we die before the Second Coming? We know that our bodies decompose. But how do our souls pass the time before Christ returns with our new flesh and bones?

The clincher may be in Revelation 6:9–10, where John said he saw "the souls of those who had been slaughtered for the word of God and for the testimony they had given." These martyrs had already died and were with God in heaven (what some would call the "intermediate" heaven since the New Heaven and Earth aren't created until later according to Revelation 21). Their souls cry out, "Sovereign Lord, holy and true, how long will it be before you judge and avenge our blood on the inhabitants of the earth?" This suggests that they know their tormentors on earth have not yet come to justice.

Does this mean that your loved ones in heaven can now see your secret sins and mourn for them? Perhaps. But remember that they are now connected with the overwhelming love and grace of God. If they are aware of your sins, they are also aware of

Heaven will be a deal more like earth than we think, and we shall not be so much altered.

Catherine Booth of the Salvation Army

their own, and they are more aware than ever that God's amazing grace covers all those sins.

We're not given as much information about this, except for one crucial fact. We will be with the Lord. Discussing his impending death, Paul said, "My desire is to depart and be with Christ, for that is far better" (Philippians 1:23). Elsewhere he equates being "away from the body" with being "at home with the Lord" (2 Corinthians 5:8). And didn't Jesus tell the thief on the cross, "Today you will be with me in Paradise" (Luke 23:43)? It's clear that the Christian soul goes immediately to the presence of the Lord, and we can certainly call this state of being "heaven."

So here's the story. When we die, our bodies return to dust, but our souls live on in heaven— some call this an "intermediate" heaven. The most important fact about this place is that God lives there. Our souls will be with God.

At some point, Christ will return to earth and our souls will return with him, inhabiting re-created bodies that are "imperishable." In these bodies, we will enjoy the blessings of the New Heaven/New Earth/New Jerusalem, as described in the Book of Revelation.

At the Last Supper, shortly before his crucifixion, Jesus told his closest disciples, "In my Father's house there are many dwelling places. If it were not so, would I have told you that I go to prepare a place for you? And if I go and prepare a place

∽∾∽∾∽∾

At some point, Christ will return to earth and our souls will return with him, inhabiting re-created bodies that are "imperishable."

∽∾∽∾∽∾

for you, I will come again and will take you to myself, so that where I am, there you may be also" (John 14:2–3).

He was probably talking about this intermediate state, rather than the New Heaven and New Earth. Notice that Jesus wasn't talking about golden streets or pearly gates, just "dwelling places." (These were translated as "mansions" in the King James Version, but they're really just homes.) The important thing to keep in mind is that we will be in heaven with him.

And how does Jesus "prepare" this place? By sweeping the floors and cleaning the counters? That's what it sounds like, doesn't it—as if he's going ahead to air out the vacation home? But it could be said that his death on the cross cleaned us, removing the stain of sin that would prevent us from dwelling at peace with God. He was going to prepare himself as the sacrifice that would pay our way into heaven.

The Waiting Room

So is this intermediate, presence-of-God heaven just a waiting room for us? Will our souls read magazines while we wait for our new, improved bodies? Don't think of it that way. After all, our souls will be fully in God's presence. Paul assures us that this state is "far better" than our earthly life.

But here's another juicy detail. Once we leave earth, we're no longer bound by time. We enter the realm of eternity. Yesterday, today, and forever all melt together. So we won't be moaning, "I've been waiting in line for a thousand years, and it looks like there's another thousand to go." In fact, the Bible

*Once we leave earth, we're no longer bound
by time. We enter the realm of eternity.*

tells us, "With the Lord one day is like a thousand years, and a thousand years are like one day" (2 Peter 3:8). One moment we will be shucking off our old dead bodies and resting with the Lord, and the next thing we know, we're getting our exciting new bodies. On earth, maybe centuries will have passed, but we will be with the Lord, beyond time.

Lord,
I don't completely get it, but maybe that's the idea. The full truth about heaven is beyond my ability to understand. I trust you to tell me what I need to know. Right now I'll rest in the knowledge that I will be with you for eternity, and that's enough for me. Thank you.

In Jesus' name. Amen.

The Blessed Hope

What the Promise of Heaven
Means to Christians

With heaven in our future, we find purpose in our earthly lives. We find hope that things will be set right, our commitment will be rewarded, and our suffering will be over. We can rest in the promise of future healing, and we dedicate ourselves to heaven's work on earth.

A dozen people got together to form a new church. They spent a lot of time composing the church's mission statement, discussing how they would worship and planning ways to invite others to join the church. But there was another matter to decide: What would the church be named?

Various options were considered, from traditional to whimsical. With the emphasis on creative worship, "New Song" as a name was suggested. Since the church would meet in a town named Voorhees, someone else came up with "Voorhees: A Jolly Good Fellowship." But then the pastor zeroed in on a simple word that worked for everyone: Hope.

The more people thought about it, the more they liked it. They especially liked that hope is appealing to non-Christians. Isn't that something everyone wants? There's so much bad news, so much negativity, that maybe a spiritual seeker would be attracted to a place called Hope. And yet it's also connected to core doctrines of the Christian faith.

The word appears throughout Scripture, expressing faith and our attitude about the future. "May

A continual looking forward to the eternal world is not as some modern people think a form of escapism or wishful thinking, but one of the things a Christian is meant to do.

C.S. Lewis

the God of hope fill you with all joy and peace in believing, so that you may abound in hope by the power of the Holy Spirit" (Romans 15:13).

And so this group was christened "Hope Church." In the following years, hundreds of people joined the original members, and their positive attitude characterized by love, joy, and especially hope, continued to grace their church.

Our relationship with the Lord gives us hope for this life and the next. Christian hope always consists of two prongs: We know that God has the power to help us in our day-to-day struggles; and we know he wants what's best for us.

Moreover, we know that we have a future that extends beyond death. Life may become difficult for us, but we believe God will make matters right— perhaps here on earth, but certainly in heaven.

"No matter how bad things get here on earth, I know we have a future in heaven," says Judy, a current member of Hope Church. She finds comfort in being able to tell her young daughter that even death would not separate them forever. "She knows I'll be in heaven, and she'll be with me again someday."

The Surety of Suffering

~~~~

*J*esus reminds us that we will suffer on earth. Sometimes we forget that he said this, but it's right there in black and white—"In this world you will have trouble. But take heart! I have overcome the world" (John 16:33 NIV). Yes, there are all sorts of preachers and authors who promise you ease and wealth if you live God's way, but that was not Jesus' message. Life will have its difficulties, but Jesus will help us overcome them.

In fact, Jesus said he has already overcome the world. Nevertheless, we won't see the full effect of his victory until he establishes the New Heaven and New Earth. Some have compared his statement to

World War II. Once the Allied forces landed at Normandy on D-Day, the tide of the war turned dramatically. You might say the victory was won on that day, but it was still more than a year before the war officially ended. In the same way, Jesus' arrival on earth and his crucifixion and resurrection—these events overcame the power of evil, but we continue to struggle with evil until the final battle is won. That's the hope we have been given.

The Book of Revelation was written for a suffering church. "I know your affliction and your poverty," the Lord says to one of the seven congregations addressed in this book (Revelation 2:9). They were being persecuted for their faith in Jesus, and they longed for the day when their suffering would be over.

For the most part, western Christians aren't persecuted for their faith these days. Some have to endure mockery or subtle discrimination, but it's a stretch to call this persecution, especially when compared

❦❦❦❦❦

Knowing that heaven awaits us, we can bring more patience to our current crises.

❦❦❦❦❦

with the difficulties faced by the church in other countries. So you're probably not suffering in the same way the church of Smyrna did at the turn of the first century.

But we do suffer the pains of human existence, the stresses of modern life, and an assortment of health issues, rocky relationships, regrets, and disappointments. We can look to the Lord for strength to deal with all those challenges, but we also look for a better life ahead. Knowing that heaven awaits us, we can bring more patience to our current crises.

A recurring theme in Psalms is the unfairness of life. The wicked prosper while the righteous languish in poverty. "I saw the prosperity of the wicked. For they have no pain; their bodies are sound and sleek. They are not in trouble as others are; they are not plagued like other people." You can almost feel the psalmist's envy. "Such are the wicked," he continues, "always at ease, they increase in riches. All in vain I have kept my heart clean and washed my hands in innocence. For all day long I have been plagued, and am punished every morning" (Psalm 73:3–5, 12–14).

We expect the God of justice to turn the tables—now! We want him to reward good behavior with financial blessings and bring ruin to wealthy sinners. But it doesn't work like that, not in this life.

Such table-turning is part of the hope of heaven. In that world, the poor who live righteously finally get rewarded, while the wealthy who made money their idol will learn that all their riches won't buy them freedom from divine prosecution. In one of Jesus' parables, it's Lazarus, the poor beggar, who lounges in heaven at Abraham's side while the rich man who ignored him in life faces fiery torment

⟨oⲟⲟⲟⲟⲟ⟩

We live in a world of wheat and weeds. God allows good and evil to live together for now, but the "harvest" is coming.

⟨oⲟⲟⲟⲟⲟ⟩

in death. Now it is the rich man who begs for Lazarus to come over with a fingertip of cool water (Luke 16:19–31).

Jesus told another parable that helps us understand this. This parable is about the harvesting of wheat. When the wheat and weeds started to come up, the servants asked the master if they should pull up the weeds. The master replied, "No; for in gathering the weeds you would uproot the wheat along with them. Let both of them grow together until the harvest; and at harvest time I will tell the reapers, 'Collect the weeds first and bind them in bundles to be burned, but gather the wheat into my barn.'" (Matthew 13:29–30). We live in a world of wheat and weeds. God allows good and evil to live side by side for now. But, never forget the "harvest" is coming.

Rewards

⌇

The hope of heaven also includes the anticipation that we will be rewarded for the God-honoring choices we made in life. "Blessed is anyone who endures temptation," says James. "Such a one has stood the test and will receive the crown of life that the Lord has promised to those who love him" (James 1:12). Peter and Paul also refer to crowns that will be given to us in heaven as rewards (1 Peter 5:4; 2 Timothy 4:8).

Is this when we finally see who wins? Will this be the way we judge who was the best Christian? "Hey, Pastor, I got 23 crowns, and you only got 20!" It will not be a holier-than-thou competition.

No, that would totally miss the point. In fact, in Revelation 4:10 we find the "elders" worshipping God by throwing their crowns before him. It's not about acquisition and competition, but about knowing that we have pleased God. You might think of these crowns as the smiles of God. The best reward is when God says to us, "Well done!"

A young choir director was working hard to prepare the church's Christmas concert. There were new songs to learn and teach, some narrations to write, and some dramatic pieces to direct. This was a volunteer position, but somehow the whole responsibility for this concert fell on him, and he took it.

He found some joy in the work, but it was also more challenging than anything he had ever done. He was taking time off from his job, and he wasn't sleeping well.

The day before the concert, he took extra time to work with one of his sopranos on a difficult solo. She was one of the wise women in the church, and

Every saint in heaven is as a flower in the garden of God, and every soul there is as a note in some concert of delightful music.

Jonathan Edwards

she had seen his extraordinary dedication over the previous months. She wished the church could pay him for all his labor, but they couldn't afford to. As she left rehearsal, she patted his wrist and said, "You know, you'll get crowns in heaven for this."

"Thank you," he smiled weakly, but inwardly he was still processing that statement. Is that supposed to make everything okay? I'm not doing this to build some heavenly portfolio. I'm doing this to serve the Lord. I don't need payment, in this world or the next. I'm just trying to make God happy, all right? So keep the crowns, and let's just get this concert over with.

You'll have to forgive this overworked musician if he had a frazzled attitude. But that night, as he tried to sleep, he thought about those crowns—and who would be granting them. Whatever those crowns would look like, it wasn't about the gold or the jewels. It was about the look on the Lord's face as he handed them over. That smile. That warm glow of appreciation. *Did I truly please you, Lord?* That would make everything worthwhile.

Many Christian workers have this same type of experience. They work tirelessly, without pay, and they don't crave any special recognition. They're just givers. But then they realize that the Lord sees their work and appreciates it. And that's a reward they'll gladly accept.

Home

"This world is not my home. I'm just a-passin' through." That old spiritual captures the biblical idea that Christians don't really belong to this world. We are just strangers in a strange land.

Hebrews 11 hails the faith of numerous Old Testament heroes, and it finds some common elements in the stories of Abel, Enoch, Abraham, Sarah, and others. "They confessed that they were strangers and foreigners on the earth ... they desire a better country, that is, a heavenly one. Therefore God is not ashamed to be called their God; indeed, he has prepared a city for them" (Hebrews 11:13, 16).

That's our situation too. We don't quite belong here. Our true home is heaven. And that gives us a whole new sense of identity. In American culture, people often identify themselves by race and nationality. They are African-American, Irish-American, or Italian-American. Maybe we should think of ourselves as heaven-American.

"Our citizenship is in heaven," Paul wrote to the Philippians, "and it is from there that we are expecting a Savior, the Lord Jesus Christ" (Philippians

3:20). The point is, our heavenly home defines us. We don't pursue the American Dream; we pursue God's dream for us. We don't need to win; we need to serve. We don't strive to get more and more; we strive to give more and more. We don't seek to indulge our physical appetites; we seek to grow in wholeness and holiness.

⸎⸎⸎⸎⸎

The heaven-minded Christian will have a sense of detachment from the strivings of this world.

⸎⸎⸎⸎⸎

It's like sitting in front of your TV, clicking through a few hundred channels and finding nothing that appeals to you. Did you ever consider that it might be because you are not "of the world," but you are merely "in the world" and heaven-bound?

Oh, you'll find glimmers of truth in this world. Paul urged us to focus on what's true, noble, excellent, wherever we find it. We can do that. But still, the heaven-minded Christian will have a sense of detachment from the strivings of this world. That can be a lonely feeling sometimes, until you realize how bright your future is. Your home is in heaven, and you'll be spending eternity there.

Values

≈≈

An old Christian chorus talked about living each day "With Eternity's Values in View." Eternity's values? What are they?

Well, you might be working for a company that does long-range planning. Rather than make decisions that will boost the bottom line for this quarter, they're looking at next year or the next decade. How can the business remain strong over the long haul?

Eternity's values are something like that, except it's ultra-long-range planning. We are looking ahead to a life in heaven, and that kind of planning shapes the decisions we make on earth. So, we could bend

the truth or cheat the tax people or slander a col-
league, and that might give us a temporary advan-
tage. But we're looking to please the Lord of
Eternity. You could win that fight with your spouse,
terrorize your kids into being quiet, and cut down
your neighbor's tree that keeps dropping acorns into
your yard. Winning like that might work for today,
but it's not the best long view—especially if that
view extends into heaven.

Jesus talked about the values that characterize
his followers: humility, meekness, peacemaking,
a hunger for what's right, and so on (Matthew
5:3–12). Each of these sounds like a bad idea if
you're looking for short-term success. But our awareness of heaven gives us the long view of life, and so
we try to live Jesus' way.

It's not easy living with godly patience in this
need-it-now world, but the hope of heaven keeps us
going. "Godliness is valuable in every way, holding
promise for both the present life and the life to

come," wrote Paul to his young friend Timothy. "To this end we toil and struggle, because we have our hope set on the living God" (1 Timothy 4:8, 10).

Healing

*A*ndrea can't wait to get her heavenly body. All her life she has been overweight. This has caused other physical problems, which have always made it hard to lose those extra pounds. She gets tired of this constant struggle, but she knows there is healing ahead. With great anticipation she reads 1 Corinthians 15, which promises that she will be "changed." She longs to put on that imperishable physique and walk the streets of glory with a body that matches her healthy soul.

She's not alone. Our earthly existence is full of disease and injury. As we age, we accumulate new pains. It gets harder and harder to walk a flight of

Is It Possible to be "So Heavenly Minded They're No Earthly Good"?

You might know some people who are always talking about heaven. They can get irritating sometimes. Why? Because it seems they never deal with the issue at hand. They don't mourn for someone's crisis; they rejoice in some eternal silver lining. They don't pray for someone's need; they thank God for the way he'll meet that need in heaven. In the words of that clever put-down, you might say they're "so heavenly minded they're no earthly good." ("No earthly good" is a bit strong, but you get the idea.)

The problem is not that they're thinking about heaven. It's that they're not connecting with earth. God doesn't want us to be wrapped up in the world's values, but he does want us to share his love with our neighbors. That means showing empathy, understanding their lives, and listening to their needs. Our heavenly perspective will always give us hope to share in dire circumstances, but we should be compassionate in the way we share our hope.

We get some solid advice from Peter: "Always be prepared to give an answer to everyone who asks you to give the reason for the hope that you have. But do this with gentleness and respect" (1 Peter 3:15 NIV). If we go through life with a heavenly hope, people will want to know why—as long as we're sharing it with gentleness and respect.

stairs, to pick up the morning paper, or even to get out of bed. We have emotional wounds too, and relationships that are deeply damaged. Some of us lose our ability to laugh or cry or say, "I'm sorry."

The promise of heaven brings the hope of healing. "We do not lose heart," Paul said. "Even though our outer nature is wasting away, our inner nature is being renewed day by day. For this slight momentary affliction is preparing us for an eternal weight of glory beyond all measure" (2 Corinthians 4:16–18).

But heaven's healing won't just affect us. The earth itself is broken and crying out for repair. "For the creation waits with eager longing for the revealing of the children of God ... in hope that the creation itself will be set free from its bondage to decay and will obtain the freedom of the glory of the children of God" (Romans 8:19–21). Paul went on to talk about creation "groaning in labor pains" just as we Christians "groan inwardly while we wait for adoption, the redemption of our bodies" (vs. 22–24).

Sometimes people blame God for the hurricanes and floods that afflict the earth, but the Bible indicates that those natural disasters are just the tantrums of a broken-down planet. Sin has damaged the entire system, which sorely needs a reboot. And that's just what the Lord has in store.

Thy Kingdom Come

Sometimes we pray for things that don't happen, and we wonder why. These prayers aren't selfish prayers. They're the sort of prayers God should want to answer. Why doesn't he honor our requests? We pray for the healing of a loved one, but that person dies. Why didn't God come through?

Well, maybe he did. Some healings he does on earth; others he does in heaven.

In the Lord's Prayer, we say, "Thy kingdom come, thy will be done, on earth as it is in heaven." We know that his heavenly kingdom has complete health and peace and all the other things we pray for. We're asking him to bring some of that into our present situation. Sometimes he agrees to do just that. Other times he asks us to wait. He will answer our prayers, but maybe on the other side of glory.

Lord,
Help me look at life with a heavenly per-
spective. Give me the hope that gets me
through each day, as I anticipate the glories
you have promised.

In Jesus' name. Amen.

God Is in His Heaven

What the Old Testament Teaches

The idea of heaven developed throughout Scripture. Ancient people assumed that God lived in the sky, and after death people went to the mysterious "place of the dead." But then the Hebrew poets and prophets began talking about an eternal existence with the Lord.

In the early 1960s, the United States strove to win the space race with the Soviet Union. Which of these two countries would be first to send a person into space? Both nations had launched spacecraft into orbit without any passengers, then they sent animals. But who would be the first human to orbit the earth? And what language would that person speak?

This race into space might have been a friendly scientific competition if it weren't for the political

climate. The Cold War was at its coldest. It was
the Communist world against the free world in
a clash of cultures, of military readiness, and of
religion.

Yes, religion. The Communist regime was
officially atheistic, denying the existence of God.
While there was some tolerance for the Eastern
Orthodox traditions, other Christian groups had
to meet in secret. Bibles were forbidden. Evangelism
was severely punished. Many Americans feared that
the growth of communism would spread atheism
throughout the world. We had to get into space
first because it wasn't just the American way
of life we were fighting for. We were fighting
for God.

And then we lost.

On April 12, 1961, Yuri A. Gagarin became
the first human in space, aboard a Soviet capsule.
Reportedly, when he entered space and looked
around, he radioed back a message that riled

What Happened to Old Testament Believers When They Died?

The Bible isn't clear about this, and so there are several theories. Since Hebrews 11 extols the faith of various Old Testament people, we know that some Hebrews had a genuine relationship with God through faith. Even though Jesus had not come yet, they trusted in God to save them, and God honors that faith. So, like Christian believers, they may have gone directly to heaven to be with God.

There's another intriguing idea, however, that's worth considering. Some suggest that since Jesus hadn't yet "paid their way" to heaven, Old Testament believers had to wait in a kind of "limbo" for Jesus to fulfill his earthly ministry. Some would say this was a soul-sleep; others consider it a place of pleasantness, but not the amazing glory of heaven.

Jesus told a story of a rich man and poor man who died. The rich man was in fiery torment, while the poor man went to "Abraham's side." There was a large chasm between the two places, but it was within speaking distance. Of course, that's a story

Jesus told—he might not be giving us the exact portrait of the afterworld.

If you accept this idea of a waiting room for Old Testament believers, that should help you interpret the strange 1 Peter 3:18–20 passage where Jesus "made a proclamation to the spirits in prison." In fact, there are various paintings from Medieval times depicting this event. They call it the "harrowing of hell," in which Jesus (in the three days between crucifixion and resurrection) stormed hell's gates and set the faithful free.

But remember the timelessness of eternity. The waiting room might not be necessary if they're in the "eternal now" of heaven.

religious folks throughout the free world. "I don't see any God up here," the cosmonaut quipped.

Maybe Gagarin thought he was scoring a point for Communist atheism. Since there was no God up there in "the heavens," he reasoned, there was no God at all. At first, Christians seemed to be irked at his insolence, but then it became apparent that he

just didn't get it. It certainly gave ministers something to preach about for a few weeks.

Where is God? From childhood we were taught
that he was "up there." But Yuri Gagarin went "up
there," and he didn't see God. What does that tell
us? Is God farther out there . . . or maybe he's farther
in here?

Perhaps some people gave up on God because
they thought he was always "up there," a place where
they never needed him. Poet Robert Browning once
wrote, "God is in his heaven and all's right with the
world." But these people saw that everything was
wrong with the world, and God seemed to be stay-
ing in his heaven. As they saw it, God just propped
up priests and coddled kings, but he remained far
away from the common people.

What Gagarin and so many other Russians and
Americans needed to know was that God doesn't
orbit the earth; he pervades it. He doesn't dwell
in the stratosphere; he takes up residence in our

Oh the delights, the heavenly joys
The glories of the place
Where Jesus sheds the brightest beams
Of his o'er flowing grace.

Isaac Watts

hearts. You won't see him on a trip into space, but you can't miss his presence when you meet a true Christian.

Seven-and-a-half years after Gagarin's space flight, there was an interesting sequel to his comment. Apollo 8 was orbiting the moon with astronauts Lovell, Anders, and Borman aboard. As they emerged from the dark side of the moon, they transmitted stunning pictures of the earth. It was Christmas 1968, and on this occasion it seemed good to these astronauts to read from the Bible.

So they read: "In the beginning, God created the heaven and the earth. . . ."

Sky and Stars

*A*s we examine what the Bible says about heaven, we need to start at the beginning. God created "the heaven." This is the Hebrew word *shamayim,* which the writers of the Old Testament used in several ways.

Have you ever wondered about that whole firmament thing? In the King James Version of the creation story (from which the astronauts read), God said, "Let there be a firmament in the midst of the waters, and let it divide the waters from the waters" (Genesis 1:6 KJV). What's a "firmament"?

The ancient Hebrews saw the blue sky and figured there was another sea up there. After all, wasn't that

Have you ever wondered about that whole firmament thing?

where rain came from? When you think about water vapor, humidity, and clouds, they weren't really wrong. So God separated the sky-sea from the water-sea with a firm atmospheric divider—different versions call it a "dome" or just an "expanse." In ancient Hebrew thinking, God put one sea above and the other below. At night, the starry sky revealed a heaven beyond the sky-sea. The creation account has God putting lights in the firmament "to divide the day from the night" (verse 14 KJV).

Heaven was understood as God's storehouse. Rain, snow, hail, and the occasional lightning bolt came from up there. It was God who sent these things, and so it only made sense that he lived up there, too. A prayer offered in Deuteronomy 26:15 says, "Look down from your holy habitation, from heaven, and bless your people Israel."

The early Israelites thought that God lived up beyond the sky. If they could ever get past that dome of a firmament, they might find him. This was the kind of thinking Yuri Gagarin mocked when he said he didn't see God when he was in space.

And yet, the Old Testament provides various pictures of God residing in the heavens. "Heaven is my throne and the earth is my footstool," the Lord declares (Isaiah 66:1). What a vivid picture! In fact, some of the psalms depict Jerusalem as God's footstool. The heavens were certainly his throne room, but the holy city was where he made contact with earth. "He who sits in the heavens laughs," said the psalmist, showing God in his front-cloud seat as he observes the follies of rebellious leaders on earth (Psalm 2:4).

But there was a problem with putting God in the heavens. The people of Canaan had a sky-god named Baal, who (in their thinking) sent rain from heaven, which kept his wife happy (the earth-goddess Asherah). Many other cultures also had this male-female, sky-earth, god-goddess duality in their religions, but the God of Israel was different. He was

Let us be content with the limits divinely set for us: namely, that the souls of the pious, having ended the toil of their warfare, enter into blessed rest, where in glad expectation they await the enjoyment of the promised glory, and so all things are held in suspense until Christ the Redeemer appears.

John Calvin
Institutes (3,25,6)

not just a rainmaker, he was Lord above all. To preserve this idea, the Israelites began talking about the "heaven of heavens" or the "highest heaven" to describe the Lord's true home.

In his wisdom, King Solomon made a brilliant statement in his dedication prayer for the Temple in Jerusalem. "Even heaven and the highest heaven cannot contain you, much less this house that I have built!" (1 Kings 8:27). This Temple was designed to be God's home on earth. At its center was the Holy of Holies, a place so sacred that only the High Priest could enter, and only once a year. The presence of the Lord was in this building, but not only in this building, Solomon said. Later in the prayer, he pleaded, "O hear in heaven your dwelling place" (verse 30). He acknowledged that God resided in heaven—but that even the highest heaven could not contain him.

"Where can I go from your spirit?" David asked. "Where can I flee from your presence? If I go up to the heavens, you are there; if I make my bed in the depths, you are there" (Psalm 139:7–8 NIV). The Lord gave the rain, but he did not just live among the clouds. He shepherded the stars out into the night sky, but he did not just live among the stars. You might speak of a third heaven, the highest heaven, as his home, but even that could not contain him. He was everywhere, high and low. When David said God is in "the depths," he talked about Sheol, the place where people go after death.

Where is God? He is in his heaven and his Temple.... He is everywhere and especially in the hearts of those humble souls who bow before him.

In Isaiah we read, "Thus says the high and lofty one who inhabits eternity, whose name is Holy: I dwell in the high and holy place, and also with those who are contrite and humble in spirit" (Isaiah 57:15). Where is God? He is in his heaven and his Temple. Perhaps we could say he is in any place where people worship him. He is everywhere and especially in the hearts of those humble souls who bow before him.

Where Do the Dead Go?

*T*here are some ideas that develop through-out Scripture, as God reveals more and more to his people. We just saw this with the idea of where God is. The same kind of development occurred with the concept of death. What happens when people die?

Nothing! That's the answer you received at first. The dead just stop living. In Hebrew thought, there was no separation of the soul from the body (a Greek idea), and so the soul died with the body and was buried with it. Hebrew writers also talked about going down to the Pit, which they called Sheol.

Death is called "the land of silence" (Psalm 94:17). There is no connection with God there, no memory of him. "For Sheol cannot thank you," says Isaiah, "death cannot praise you; those who go down to the Pit cannot hope for your faithfulness" (Isaiah 38:18).

You might expect that only bad people would go to the Pit, but that's not the way it worked. In a few special cases, Enoch and Elijah had a direct route to heaven, but in general you were either living or dead, and living was preferable. "A living dog is better than a dead lion," growled the Preacher of Ecclesiastes. "The living know that they will die, but the dead know nothing; they have no more reward, and even the memory of them is lost" (Ecclesiastes 9:4–5).

But soon there were whispers of hope. Maybe death wasn't the end. Maybe God could reach even into the grave.

Poor Job had lost everything and was scraping boils from his skin. Still he mustered the faith to say, "I know that my Redeemer lives, and that at the last he will stand upon the earth; and after my skin has been thus destroyed, then in my flesh I shall see God" (Job 19:25–26).

In Psalm 16, David spoke of a kind of resurrection. "Therefore my heart is glad, and my soul rejoices; my body also rests secure. For you do not give me up to Sheol or let your faithful one see the Pit. You show me the path of life. In your presence

⋙⋘⋙⋘⋙⋘

Several biblical writers were sick and tired of watching the wicked get away with murder while poor believers suffered.

⋙⋘⋙⋘⋙⋘

there is fullness of joy; in your right hand are pleasures forevermore" (Psalm 16:9–11). Simon Peter used this verse in his Pentecost sermon as a prophecy about Jesus (Acts 2:25–28). It certainly works that way, but it also hints at a future resurrection for every "faithful one" who dies.

Suddenly there was a new hope for divine justice. Several biblical writers were sick and tired of watching the wicked get away with murder while poor believers suffered. Now they saw that God could make things right in the afterlife.

Asaph, the author of Psalm 73, raged against the prosperity of the wicked "till I entered the sanctuary of God; then I understood their final destiny. Surely you place them on slippery ground; you cast them down to ruin." They are ultimately doomed to the

Pit, and God's judgment. By contrast, Asaph noted, "Yet I am always with you; you hold me by my right hand. You guide me with your counsel, and afterward you will take me into glory" (Psalm 73:17–18, 23–24 NIV). God's presence is an eternal blessing for a righteous soul like Asaph.

As Paul confirmed in the New Testament, God would raise everyone for a final judgment.

So, somewhere along the line, Sheol got subdivided. Everyone still went to the Pit after death, but the righteous had the hope of rising into God's presence. A later prophecy made this explicit: "Many of those who sleep in the dust of the earth shall awake, some to everlasting life, and some to shame and everlasting contempt" (Daniel 12:2). Finally, the end-time resurrection is revealed! As Paul confirmed in the New Testament, God would raise everyone for a final judgment.

New Things

There was another question nagging at the hearts of the faithful. What was God doing on earth? With nation rising against nation, and with Gentiles oppressing God's chosen people, what would become of this planet?

Israel had briefly enjoyed political power in their corner of the world. David had won it, and Solomon used it to expand his empire. But the fortunes of God's people had tumbled since those glory days. A succession of superpowers had marched in to enslave the Israelites. Was there any hope for the nation? Was there any hope for the world?

Yes, for the Hebrew prophets unleashed a fresh vision of God's designs. Indeed the prophet Ezekiel saw a valley of dry bones coming back to life. Sounds like a horror flick, doesn't it? But this was a picture of God's redemption. "I am going to open

Will We Be Judged for the Works We Have Done?

Some Old Testament passages seem to say our eternal destiny is based on the good or bad works we do. Many people today believe that. The New Testament, on the other hand, is quite clear that we are saved "by grace ... through faith ... not the result of works" (Ephesians 2:8–9).

Can both be true? Yes, they can. Let's look at how they can be.

In our own power, we cannot be righteous enough to earn our way to heaven. We all are sinners. We must trust Christ to save us from our sin. When we do, we tap into God's power to do good works. Our righteous lives are the proof that we have trusted in the Lord. So good works and grace are inseparable.

In the Old Testament, those who trusted God tried to follow God's law. Those who refused to trust God lived by their own rules. And there were always those—like the enemies of the prophet Jeremiah, some of the Pharisees of Jesus' day, and some folks today—who claimed to keep God's law letter-perfect, but the loveless way they have lived reveal their lack of true faith.

True righteousness follows true faith, and the connection is strong. In Jesus' name, God will dispense a lot of grace on Judgment Day as we sinners bow humbly before him. If we rely on our own goodness, we'll fall short. If we rely on his goodness—that's our in.

The New Testament also suggests that there may be a later evaluation of the actions of believers—sometimes called "the Judgment Seat of Christ" (Romans 14:10; 1 Corinthians 3:11–15; 2 Corinthians 5:10). At this point, we're already in heaven to stay, but we're called to give account for our actions. Presumably this is where we win crown-rewards, which we would offer back to Christ in humility and gratitude.

your graves, and bring you up from your graves, O my people . . . I will put my spirit within you, and you shall live" (Ezekiel 37:12, 14).

As Isaiah saw it, however, not just the nation but all of creation was up for renewal. "I am about to

⋙⋙⋘⋘

*Not just the nation but all of
creation was up for renewal.*

⋙⋙⋘⋘

create new heavens and a new earth," the Lord said,
adding, "I am about to create Jerusalem as a joy . . .
no more shall the sound of weeping be heard in it,
or the cry of distress" (Isaiah 65:17–19).

This was the beginning of a promise that New
Testament writers would pick up. God was going to
remake things, and the faithful would live forever
with him in this joy-filled place.

Lord,
I worship you as the God of highest heaven,
but I thank you for coming to my level.
Help me see your heavenly presence in my
earthly life.

In Jesus' name. Amen.

Kingdom Come

Jesus' Teaching About Heaven

Jesus spoke of the "kingdom of heaven" as something both now and later, both earthly and divine. But more importantly, he promised to "prepare a place" in heaven for his followers after his earthly ministry.

"The king is dead! Long live the king!"

They say bewildering things like that in children's fairy tales in which a power shift is proclaimed at the beginning or end of the story. Such statements can be confusing to children. "Is the king dead or alive?" Some kids go years before they get it. "Oh!" they finally realize, "the *old* king is dead, and the people want the *new* king to live a long time."

That's the kind of message we hear at the beginning of Jesus' earthly ministry. The first public announcement he made was about a new kingdom.

"Repent," he said, "for the kingdom of heaven has come near."

The old kingdom of earth is *over*. Now there's a new king, and his kingdom is replacing the old kingdom of earth.

The Near Kingdom

The kingdom of heaven was one of Jesus' favorite topics. Read his words in the gospels, and you'll see how often he talked about heaven. Of course, he frequently spoke of love, and surprisingly, he talked a great deal about money. But he referred to God's kingdom more often. Again and again he started his stories by saying, "The kingdom of heaven is like ... " (e.g., see Matthew 13:31, 33).

A note on the language: In the Gospel of Luke, Jesus spoke of the kingdom of *God*. Because Matthew displays a traditional Hebrew reluctance to say

Will We Recognize One Another in Heaven?

Yes, but in a different way. The best evidence comes from Jesus' experience after his resurrection. We are assuming, from Paul's teaching, that our resurrection bodies will be something like Christ's resurrection body. Did his friends recognize him? Yes, they did . . . eventually.

Mary Magdalene first mistook the risen Jesus for a gardener, but after he spoke her name, she recognized him (John 20:11–18).

Later, Jesus met a number of disciples as they were fishing on the Sea of Galilee. As he called to them from the shore, they didn't recognize him, but when he worked a miracle, they did (John 21:1–8).

Jesus also appeared to his disciples in a house and showed them the wounds in his hands and side (John 20:19–29), the same wounds he had received when the Romans crucified him. Thomas (and perhaps the others) did not accept Jesus' identity from his appearance alone—until he saw the scars from those wounds.

> In each encounter, Jesus' appearance alone was not enough, but there was some personal factor that confirmed Jesus' identity—his caring voice, his miraculous power, his sacrificial wounds. These factors were intrinsic to his true identity, and thus his loved ones recognized him at a deeper level.
>
> That suggests that our encounters in heaven will not be based solely on appearance but on deeper personal factors. And just as we will recognize Jesus, we *will* know one another.

the holy name of God, he has Jesus preaching about the kingdom of *heaven* in his Gospel account. But in reality, it's the same thing. Today, when we say, "Heaven help us" we're really talking about God's help. As we've already seen, since heaven is the very presence of God, the word heaven is a fitting replacement. Perhaps Matthew gets us thinking about heaven and earth or about heaven *on* earth, and that's a good thing.

In heaven, God is king. No question about that. Angels praise him; saints adore him. His words are law. But earth is a different story. While God certainly has ultimate power, many people ignore him and his will. The Bible refers to the devil as "the ruler of the power of the air" (Ephesians 2:2), indicating that he has power over us—at least to some extent.

But then Jesus showed up announcing that the kingdom of heaven was drawing near. What did he mean by that?

For one thing, he meant that events were about to happen that would pave the way to heaven. In about three years Jesus would sacrifice his life, offering atonement for our sins. From the very start, this was his destination. Indeed, John the Baptist prophetically called Jesus "the [sacrificial] Lamb of God who takes away the sin of the world!" (John 1:29).

Jesus also taught that the kingdom of heaven is *accessible*. It is within reach of all his followers. For too long the religious elite had made it difficult to know God, and Jesus came to change that.

❦❦❦❦

We try to live each day in a heavenly way although we know the full glories of heaven still await us.

❦❦❦❦

And don't miss the irony of who was announcing the nearness of the kingdom. King Jesus himself! "My kingdom is not from this world," he later told Pilate at his trial (John 18:36). The kingdom of heaven is also *his* kingdom. So when Jesus said it was "near," well, it was standing right in front of them—in his own person.

That simple word *near* is delightfully ambiguous. It carries ideas of both present and future. In other words, the kingdom that Jesus offered had already arrived—in Jesus—but it was not yet fully complete. And isn't that what we're finding out about heaven? As believers, we have an eternal life that starts right now on earth. We try to live each day in a heavenly way although we know the full glories of heaven still await us.

The Turnabout Kingdom

*esus said heaven is "near"—about to happen, accessible, already and not yet. But what else did Jesus say about the kingdom of heaven? More specifically, what kind of kingdom did Jesus say it would be?

It would be a place of turnabout. Those who were persecuted on earth would have great rewards in heaven. The kingdom of heaven belonged to the "poor in spirit"—that is, the humble (Matthew 5:3). Those who exalted themselves will experience an embarrassing fall. Those who wielded power will have to give account before God. The rich will not be able to lug their possessions into the next life.

Picking up a theme from the psalms and the prophets, Jesus elaborated on this truth. According to David, Asaph, Isaiah, and Jeremiah, life on earth just isn't fair. The wicked prosper, and the righteous suffer—and that stinks. But Jesus brought the clearest picture yet of the redemption that heaven will bring. That's where the wicked will have to pay up, and the righteous will be rewarded.

◆◆◆◆◆

Would you rather live it up for your seventy-odd years of earthly life or for the endless ages in the kingdom of heaven?

◆◆◆◆◆

Suddenly it all made sense. When you enlarge your field of vision to include the afterlife, righteousness becomes your best option by far. After all, would you rather live it up for your seventy-odd years of earthly life or for the endless ages in the kingdom of heaven?

We see this turnabout most vividly in Jesus' story of the rich man and a beggar named Lazarus (Luke 16:19–31). After a lifetime of ignoring the poor beggar, the rich man dies—and so does the beggar. The next scene occurs in Sheol, the place of the dead. No longer pampered, the rich man is writhing in fiery agony while the beggar lounges comfortably at Abraham's side.

This picture of the afterlife would have been familiar to the Jews of Jesus' day. It is not necessarily a precise blueprint of the afterworld. Jesus might have been using a commonly accepted scene in order to make his point—or he could have been describing the real situation of believers from the Old Testament era.

At this point, many people assumed that the righteous would go to a place of pleasantness after death and the wicked would suffer in Sheol, or hell. The shocking thing about Jesus' parable is that the rich man goes to the place of the wicked. And why? Because he ignored the needs of this poor beggar.

With poetic irony, Jesus has the rich man begging for the ex-beggar. "He called out, 'Father Abraham, have mercy on me, and send Lazarus to dip the tip of his finger in water and cool my tongue; for I am in agony in these flames.'" (verse 24).

In reply, Abraham spells out the turnabout. The rich man had "received good things" during his lifetime, and Lazarus had received "evil things" (verse 25). Now it was going to be the other way around.

This role reversal seems to catch the rich man by surprise, which furthers the notion that he wasn't really a bad guy, just a bit tight-fisted. He begs Abraham to send Lazarus to warn his five brothers. Presumably they are also rich, and they have no clue of the torment awaiting them. "They have Moses and the prophets," Abraham answers (verse 29). "They should listen to them."

This idea of caring for the poor wasn't new. It appears in the law of Moses and often in the prophetic writings, but apparently for these privileged souls the lure of wealth carried more weight than the clear teaching of Scripture.

Investing in the Future

Sometimes it seems that Jesus is anti-money. That's not really true. Jesus knows that money has its place in our lives, but what he was warning us against is the love of money, which can keep people out of heaven. For many, many people, it's an either/or situation. Money has a way of demanding our attention, insisting on more and more allegiance from us. "No one can serve two masters," Jesus warned. "You cannot serve God and wealth" (Matthew 6:24).

So if you have money, how do you keep it from sabotaging your heavenly future? First, by recognizing that you can't take it with you. In another parable, Jesus mocked a rich fool whose crops were so plentiful he kept tearing down his barns and building bigger ones. "Eat, drink, and be merry" was this guy's motto. "But God said to him, 'You fool! This very night your life is being demanded of you. And the things you have prepared, whose will they be?'" (Luke 12:19–20).

Also, recognize your obligation to care for the poor. The New Testament speaks with honor of a few wealthy folks who subsidized the ministry of Jesus, Paul, and others; obviously this would be another outlet for your funds. Perhaps more than anything, you need to avoid trusting in your money for your happiness and peace of mind. Instead, those things (peace and happiness) come when you give to those who are in need.

Jesus urged his followers to make investments not on earth but in heaven (Matthew 6:19–21). How do we do that? By holding heavenly priorities in our hearts. "Where your treasure is, there your heart will

Put your treasure in heaven by putting your heart there. Care about the things God cares about.

be also," Jesus said (verse 21), and that could probably work in the other way as well. Put your treasure
in heaven by putting your heart there. Care about
the things God cares about.

Right off the bat, in his Sermon on the Mount,
Jesus listed eight qualities that will win rewards from
God. These characteristics would hardly qualify as
get-rich-quick schemes: humility, mourning, meekness, a desire for justice, mercy, pure motives, peacemaking, and accepting persecution for doing right.
In fact, they might be get-*poor*-quick strategies, if
we're talking about earthly wealth. But these are all
ways of connecting with the heart of God, and he
promises a heavenly payoff on these investments.

Maybe you've already had to get serious about
investing in a retirement plan. It's tough to put aside
that extra sum each month for an IRA or a 401K
plan, but it's wise to plan for the future. Jesus often
made that same point, except the "future" for him
lasted forever.

In one of his strangest parables, Jesus commended a dishonest businessman. This middle manager got fired, but he still had a few days remaining on the job. So he used his lame-duck position to call in his company's debtors and offer them deals to erase their debts. Possibly he was hoping that one of the recipients of these favors might provide him with a new job.

Jesus certainly didn't approve the middle manager's dishonesty, but he commended his foresight. The manager was making plans for his future—as we should. "I tell you," Jesus said, "use worldly wealth to gain friends for yourselves, so that when it is gone, you will be welcomed into eternal dwellings" (Luke 16:9 NIV). Our time employed in earthly pursuits is coming to an end. Therefore, we should use our current resources to prepare for our heavenly future.

Surprise!

*A*nother recurring theme in Jesus' teaching about heaven is surprise. In several of his stories, people seem surprised at who is in heaven, who's not in heaven, and why. "Not everyone who says to me, 'Lord, Lord,' will enter the kingdom of heaven, but only the one who does the will of my Father in heaven" (Matthew 7:21). Was Jesus preaching some sort of salvation-by-works? No. The "will of the Father" is to respond in faith to Christ. That response is both a heart commitment and a life commitment. Elsewhere Jesus said, "This is the work of God, that you believe in him whom he has sent" (John 6:29). Here he's contrasting those who talk a good game with those who mean it. Eternal life is not for those who follow their own agenda and say they're doing it for Christ. It's for those who bow before the Lord and seek to do what he wants.

The same idea occurs in an extended parable Jesus told late in his ministry. The main character is the Son of Man who appears in glory and then assumes his throne. He proceeds to sit in judgment over the "nations"—the people of the whole world.

Eternal life is not for those who follow their own agenda and say they're doing it for Christ. It's for those who bow before the Lord and seek to do what he wants.

Who is this person? Of course, it's Jesus himself. He often used the term Son of Man for himself, borrowing it from the Old Testament. The prophet Ezekiel used that title in humility to mean "mere human," and Jesus probably adopted it as an indication of his own humble service.

But another prophet, Daniel, also used the term, seeing "one like a son of man, coming with the clouds of heaven" (Daniel 7:13 NIV). In Daniel's end-time vision, this Son of Man receives authority from the "Ancient of Days" (obviously the Creator, the Father). This was exactly the picture Jesus needed to describe his own identity and mission. He was the Son, empowered by the Father.

Throughout his ministry, Jesus exemplified the double meaning of Son of Man—humble and yet divine, but at his trial, Jesus no longer needed to hide its meaning. Asked point blank if he was the Messiah, Jesus said, "I am; and you will see the Son of Man seated at the right hand of the Power, and 'coming with the clouds of heaven'" (Mark 14:62). It was Daniel's vision, which Jesus now fully claimed.

He told the parable just days before that trial, and here the Son of Man is appearing and reigning, *a la* Daniel's prophecy. As the nations come before him, he divides up the people as a shepherd separates sheep from goats. One group is welcomed into eternal bliss while the other is cast off into eternal fire.

On what basis is this decision made? "I was hungry and you gave me food," says the Son of Man to the blessed ones. "I was thirsty and you gave me something to drink, I was a stranger and you welcomed me, I was naked and you gave me clothing, I was sick and you took care of me, I was in prison and you visited me" (Matthew 25:35).

The listeners are stunned. As they see it, the records must be wrong. All those situations never happened to them. They never saw the Son of Man in need and helped him. They wonder aloud, *When exactly was this?*

⌒⌒⌒

If I ever reach heaven I expect to find three wonders there: first, to meet some I had not thought to see there; second, to miss some I had expected to see there; and third, the greatest wonder of all, to find myself there.

John Newton

The Son of Man answers, "Truly I tell you, just as you did it to one of the least of these who are members of my family, you did it to me" (verse 40).

Imagine the delightful surprise of someone who gains an eternal reward because she bought a sandwich for a beggar or he wrote letters to prison inmates. She was just meeting a need. He was just trying to help out. No big deal. But the Lord honors those simple graces, as if they were offered directly to him.

Jesus then retold the story on the negative side. Those who are doomed to punishment are equally shocked to learn that ignoring the needy was tantamount to ignoring the Son himself. That doesn't need to scare us, but it should motivate us. Don't rely on your reputation or religious standing to unlock the gates of heaven. Is your heart open to the Lord's heart? Do you care about what he cares about? Are you humble enough to serve him and his people?

Throughout his ministry Jesus was pushing this humility of heart. Will you bow to receive God's grace and share it with others? If so, then the blessings of heaven will shower upon you.

Preparing a Place

*I*t's hard for us to imagine the tensions swirling around Jesus and his disciples in the days before his crucifixion. They were wanted men, skulking around Jerusalem, relying on secret codes to find a place to eat the Passover meal. Jesus had predicted that he would be arrested and executed, and he refused to consider otherwise. As they met for that Passover celebration, they should have known their three-year adventure was nearly over.

In that context, Jesus urged his disciples to trust him. He said, "Do not let your hearts be troubled" (John 14:1).

Trust him? He has led them right into the lion's mouth! Trust him? He has already announced that he would die in this city! Trust him for what? How could their hearts not be troubled?

But then Jesus expanded their minds. Don't just think about earth; think about heaven.

☙☙☙

Thus I believe, thus I affirm, thus I am certain it is: that from this life I shall pass to another better.

Dante

"In my Father's house there are many dwelling places," Jesus told them. "If it were not so, would I have told you that I go to prepare a place for you? And if I go and prepare a place for you, I will come again and will take you to myself, so that where I am, there you may be also" (John 14:2–3).

How would you feel in that moment? Could this adventure be over, and now there's something new ahead? Was Jesus going away, and yet he would come back to get them?

"And you know the way to the place where I am going," Jesus added (verse 5).

It was Thomas who dared to disagree. "No, Jesus, we don't understand. You're talking about preparing rooms in your Father's house. How can we possibly know how to get there?" Jesus was talking as if he was merely stepping across the street for a newspaper and a bagel, as if he'd be right over there if they needed him. But they all sensed he was going to die. He was crossing over a great divide. The Greeks wrote myths about that long and arduous journey, but now Jesus was treating it like a morning errand. No, Jesus, it *is* a big deal! Thankfully, Thomas puts our doubts into words. "Where you're going, Jesus, we've never been. How can we know the way?"

"I am the way," Jesus answered. He went on to say some great things about himself and his Father, but this simple statement is Heaven 101. Whatever else heaven is or isn't, in dreams or theology, it's all about Jesus. There were many things the disciples didn't know about heaven as they reclined at that dinner table, but they knew Jesus, and that was enough.

Lord,

I pray this with you: "Thy kingdom come, Thy will be done, on earth as it is in heaven." Let me be part of the answer to that prayer as I live my life today. Help me demonstrate what your kingdom is like so I may be a light to this world.

In Jesus' name. Amen.

Heavenly Bodies

Paul's Teaching About the Afterlife

The apostle Paul built upon Jesus' teaching on heaven by saying Christians are citizens of heaven, a place Christians should look forward to in the same way a person looks forward to going home. Moreover, Paul wrote to the Christians in Corinth that we will live our eternal lives in "imperishable" resurrected bodies, not as formless spirits. Paul foresaw the final resurrection as a redemption of the entire created order, which, according to Scripture, waits with us, indeed, groans for that glorious day.

Kaye, an aspiring actress living in New York City, was traveling to be with her family for the holidays. Her brother picked her up at their midwestern airport.

"How's everything in the Big Apple, Kaye?" he asked casually.

"Fine," she said. "It took some getting used to, but I guess I'm starting to think like a New Yorker." Just then the traffic came to a stop. The single lane leading out of the airport was blocked by a big truck, which had stopped for no apparent reason.

Her brother sat patiently behind the wheel. *Maybe they're lost,* he wondered. *Maybe they're checking a map.* But the New York actress hopped out of the car and strode up beside the stopped truck. She put a hand on her hip and called up to the driver, "So, you gonna move this thing or what?"

Yeah, her brother thought. *She's a New Yorker now.*

Places have character, and the people who lived in these places can't help but adopt it. If you're from the South, you talk a certain way. If you're from Los Angeles, you walk a certain way. If you're from New England, you think a certain way. There are always exceptions to the stereotypes of course, but the fact remains, people often assume the characteristics of their home turf.

Paul saw the same thing happening to those who were too much at home on planet Earth. "Their god is the belly; and their glory is in their shame; their minds are set on earthly things." Then he reminds them, "our citizenship is in heaven, and it is from there that we are expecting a Savior" (Philippians 3:19–20).

Did Paul Go to Heaven and Come Back?

Possibly. Paul related a strange story about someone he knew who had been taken up to the third heaven (2 Corinthians 12:1–5). That "third heaven" probably refers to the Old Testament understanding of heaven as (1) sky, (2) space, and (3) God's home—the third heaven is simply a place where God dwells.

So who was this person to whom he referred? Putting together his knowledge of the situation and the way he discussed it, with his refusal to "boast" about it—it makes sense that he was talking about himself. Otherwise, why would he consider it boasting? Paul belittled the "false apostles" in Corinth who were bragging about their own visions. "If that's what impresses you," Paul was saying, "I had a vision, too, but I hesitate to talk about it."

Or was Paul referring to a near-death experience that occurred when he was knocked to the ground on the road to Damascus (see Acts 9:1–4)? Good guess, but the timing doesn't work out right. He wrote about this event around 55 A.D., and he says the experience occurred "fourteen years ago." His conversion was around 35 A.D.

Was this then an experience he had while engaged in private worship? Possibly. We can make all sorts of guesses, but the answer is, we just don't know.

"If with Christ you died to the elemental spirits of the universe, ... if you have been raised with Christ," Paul said in yet another letter, "seek the things that are above, where Christ is, seated at the right hand of God. Set your minds on things that are above, not on things that are on earth, for you have died, and your life is hidden with Christ in God" (Colossians 2:20; 3:1–3).

We are Heaven People. Our Savior is coming from there and will take us back there. Meanwhile, live by the principles of heaven. That fact transforms our attitude. It undergirds our character. It frames our choices. It's who we are.

Our Identity in Christ

*J*esus took the Old Testament prophecies about heaven to a new level when he preached about the Kingdom of Heaven and revealed glimpses of the life beyond. The apostle Paul took Jesus' teaching, along with the events of Jesus' life, and explained it even further. The same

We are Heaven People. . . . That fact transforms our attitude. It undergirds our character. It frames our choices. It's who we are.

themes are there—the Kingdom, the Resurrection, the Redemption of All Things. Jesus had called his disciples to follow him in life; now Paul called Christians to follow Jesus into death, resurrection, and eternal life.

<hr/>

We will be given resurrection bodies like his post-resurrection body, and we will be united with him in glory.

<hr/>

Paul regularly reminds us that we go with Christ on his entire journey. We are crucified with him as we claim his death to pay for our sins. We are risen with him to a new kind of life, empowered by his spirit. We will be given resurrection bodies like his post-resurrection body, and we will be united with him in glory. One of Paul's favorite phrases is "in Christ," and now we see why. In Paul's thinking, we're not just *with* Jesus but *in* Jesus.

If you are "in Christ," Paul said, you are a new creation (2 Corinthians 5:17), created in Christ to do good works (Ephesians 2:10). If you are in Christ, you will not face condemnation for sin (Romans 8:1). In Christ you'll find grace and faith and love and encouragement. Paul explained the secret of the universe, the theory of everything, "the mystery that has been hidden throughout the ages . . . but has now been revealed." So what is it? It is "Christ in you, the hope of glory" (Colossians 1:26–27).

Jesus had prayed for this unity after the Last Supper. "As you, Father, are in me and I am in you, may they also be in us . . . I in them and you in me, that they may become completely one" (John 17:21, 23). This concept forms the core of Paul's teaching about heaven. We are to be *in* Christ.

Toward the end of his life, Paul described his dilemma. Should he wish to live or to die? He hoped that "Christ will be exalted now as always in my body, whether by life or by death," and then he put it succinctly: "For to me, living is Christ and dying is gain" (Philippians 1:20–21). It's interesting that he doesn't say that living is *for* Christ or *with* Christ. His life *is* Christ. Jesus is alive in him.

∽∾∽∾∽∾

You are already in Christ.

∽∾∽∾∽∾

That's the story for every Christian—that very title means "Christ-one." In fact, as we look forward to this world's exciting conclusion, Paul tells us, "When Christ who is your life is revealed, then you also will be revealed with him in glory" (Colossians 3:4).

Don't look at heaven as some big adjustment. Don't let its unfamiliarity scare you. According to Paul, you are already in Christ. That is your true nature. And heaven is your true home.

Resurrection

～

The Christians in Corinth gave Paul fits. They had one question after another, and whenever Paul thought he had answered one, they second-guessed him. One issue concerned various factions in the church who claimed allegiance to different outside Christian leaders. To compound the problem so-called "superapostles" blew into town and bad-mouthed Paul's reputation at every opportunity.

As you read his first letter to the Corinthians, you can hear Paul addressing question by question: church discipline, Christian liberty, and speaking in tongues, to name a few. Most of these were practical issues of church policy or personal behavior. He saved the theological question for last: Resurrection.

It wasn't the resurrection of Christ they were doubting; it was the resurrection of the body. Will

If We Die and Go to Heaven, Will We Have Bodies While We Wait for the Final Resurrection?

Good question, but there's no definitive answer. We've already talked about the "intermediate heaven" where we wait (in God's presence) for the resurrection of our bodies and the New Heaven and New Earth (see page 39). We also suggested that in the timelessness of eternity, the whole concept of "waiting" might be irrelevant.

If there is any sort of waiting, however, some wonder whether we get "intermediate bodies" for that period. Some say 2 Corinthians 5:3 indicates that we won't be "naked"—that is, bodiless—when we go to be with the Lord. Others say this verse reveals Paul's uncertainty. Some assume that our spirits must always have bodies of some sort.

Revelation 6:11 shows martyrs in heaven waiting for the final fulfillment. "They were each given a white robe and told to rest a little longer." That is one picture of believers receiving an intermediate body, which gives us some indication of our future state.

God really give us new bodies for a heavenly here-
after? It's not a crazy question. Many people today
assume that heaven is a place for disembodied spirits. Our bodies die, they say, but our spirits live on.
That may be a nice way to think, but it's not what
the Bible teaches.

In Corinth, just down the road from Athens,
Greek philosophy strongly influenced the citizens
of that town. Several centuries earlier, an Athenian
philosopher named Plato shared his theories that
divided spirit from body: the spiritual is eternal,
what's really real while the physical is a bad imitation
of that sublime ideal.

In Acts 17:16–35, we read about Paul mixing it
up with the Greek philosophers (Stoics and Epi-
cureans). They invited Paul to speak in front of the
Areopagus because they were interested in his new
teaching about the Holy Spirit's bringing true
life to our fleshly existence. At first many of these
philosopher-types eagerly accepted the message.

But why did he have to add that stuff about the resurrection of the body? That was a turnoff to Platonists. They enjoyed hearing his thoughts about Jesus—until he mentioned the resurrection (Acts 17:31–32).

So now Paul wrote to the Corinthians, responding to the heretical teachings of the nearby philosophers who were causing dissension and who had been insisting that there is no physical resurrection. They were saying spirits live but bodies die.

Like a good lawyer does, Paul crafted his argument. If there is no resurrection, then Jesus didn't rise from the dead. And if he didn't rise, then in what are we Christians believing? Without his resurrection, our faith is in trouble.

But Christ did rise from the dead as the "first fruit"—explained in Leviticus 23. He was referring to the Jewish tradition in which the first crops of each season were offered to God as a way of dedicating the entire crop. Jesus gave us a strikingly visual metaphor. Christ is the first out of the ground, and we will follow.

How is it possible that our decaying bodies would come back to life? Paul countered this objection by referring to seeds that are planted. They completely change their form! The seed dies, but a new stalk comes up. The grain that grows on the stalk doesn't look like the seed; it's a whole new thing. "So it is with the resurrection of the dead," Paul argued. "What is sown is perishable, what is raised is imperishable" (1 Corinthians 15:42).

At this point Paul described an amazing future scene, saying, "Listen, I will tell you a mystery! We will not all die, but we will all be changed, in a moment, in the twinkling of an eye, at the last trumpet. For the trumpet will sound, and the dead

I believe in the resurrection of the body.
Apostles' Creed

will be raised imperishable, and we will be changed"
(1 Corinthians 15:51–52).

Some people think that truth can only pertain to
the spiritual realm. And they look down on those
whose beliefs about God, heaven, or humanity seem
too physical or literal to them. That happened at the
church in Corinth, and it happens today. But Paul
didn't buy that erroneous outlook. Yes, he's well
aware of the spiritual struggles we have. He spent
pages urging us to let God's Spirit override our
worldly desires. But the answer isn't to ignore the
physical world.

Paul was anchored in an awareness of a God who
loves the physical world, who created it, and who
entered it in order to redeem it. Redemption is a
palpable thing. It's not a matter of setting the spirit
free from the body, but letting God's Spirit breathe
new life into our bodies while transforming it into a
whole new kind of physical being.

All Groan Up

"Repent! Entropy is increasing!" Young Steve laughed hard at this joke he had just created. He was a brilliant high school student, and no one else was smart enough to laugh with him. He tried for half an hour to explain himself, but at a certain point, if you have to work that hard to understand a joke, it's not really a joke.

In physics class, Steve had just learned about entropy. In basic terms, it is a state of disorder, and many scientists believe the universe began with low entropy. That means we started with very well-ordered energy, and we've been steadily moving toward disorder ever since. Steve was right. Entropy is increasing.

Can you apply Steve's theory to yourself? Is your life getting more chaotic every day?

The apostle Paul would agree with that idea. In several passages he described the increasing disorder of our world as the end nears. "In the last days distressing times will come," he warned his protégé Timothy (2 Timothy 3:1).

But the disorder is not just a matter of declining social morality. The whole universe is in need of redemption.

"For the creation waits with eager longing for the revealing of the children of God" (Romans 8:19). Here we see Paul's spiritual-physical connection again. When God takes us to our heavenly home, it won't be just a transfer of spirit-energy. It will be the unveiling of our new glorious bodies, as well as the creation of a new heaven and earth. We are in this together with the universe. Our redemption

Earth breaks up, time drops away
In flows heaven, with its new day
Robert Browning

❦❦❦❦❦

Then shall all the trees of the forest sing for
joy before the Lord; for he is coming.
Psalm 96:12–13

❦❦❦❦❦

will help bring about the redemption to the
created order.

"We know," said Paul, "that the whole creation
has been groaning in labor pains until now; and not
only the creation, but we ourselves, who have the
first fruits of the Spirit, groan inwardly while we
wait for adoption, the redemption of our bodies"
(Romans 8:22–23).

Paul wasn't making this up. It fits hand in glove
with Isaiah's prophecies about a new creation
(65:17) and with Jesus' warnings about famines and
earthquakes (see Matthew 24:7–8). Furthermore,
perhaps the psalmist wasn't just using poetic license
when he talked about trees singing to welcome the
Lord's coming (Psalm 96:12–13).

The creation is "subjected to futility," Paul said, but there is hope "that the creation itself will be set free from its bondage to decay and will obtain the freedom of the glory of the children of God" (Romans 8:21). Bondage to decay? That sounds a lot like entropy, an ever-increasing disorder. But then comes the event that those physicists haven't foreseen—freedom from decay, the redemption of all creation, the ultimate glory into which God will welcome us. All our groaning is forgotten as we enjoy life the way it was meant to be.

Lord,
With all creation, I look forward to the day
of redemption. Come quickly, Lord Jesus,
and remake this universe and remake me.
In Jesus' name. Amen.

The New Jerusalem

John's Vision of the Next World

The rest of the New Testament offers glimpses into the afterlife, showing it to be a place of rest from our struggles and where we will finally see Christ as he truly is. But nothing can match John's glorious vision in the Book of Revelation. We've spent far too much time debating the details of when and how we'll get there and not enough time just gazing into our future home.

"It's Friday!" the preacher crowed. "But Sunday's comin'!"

At first, the congregation wondered what he was getting at.

"It's Friday!" he repeated, and then he got a few "Amens" in response. "But Sunday's comin'!"

There was such joy in his delivery, the people perked up.

Why Is It Taking So Long for Jesus to Return?

In God's timing, it's not long at all. As we learn in 2 Peter 3:8, to God a thousand years is like a day. So it's been ... what? ... two days. Some would say he's waiting for us to bring the gospel to every nation, fulfilling the Great Commission (Matthew 28:19–20). Others have suggested other quotas or events he's waiting for. But in general, let's just allow God to set his own timetable. Rest assured that he hasn't forgotten us.

"It's Friday!" he said again, and the church swelled with agreement. "But Sunnnn-day's a-comin'!"

He stretched out every phoneme in every word of this simple phrase. And each time he repeated it, more of his listeners caught on. Soon there were shouts of "Hallelujah" greeting each phrase, as well as "Thank you, Jesus!" These people knew they were living their lives on Good Friday, dying with Christ each day as they tried to honor him in a difficult world. And they desperately wanted to hear the promise of resurrection. Sunday is coming! Easter Sunday will dawn with a whole new kind of life. We will be raised with Christ, victorious. We will enter his rest.

City Lights

We don't know who wrote the Letter to the Hebrews. It could have been Barnabas, Silas, or Priscilla. The book has the feel of a sermon, with one central theme: *Jesus fulfilled Hebrew prophecies.* Hebrews takes specific elements of the Old Testament and shows how they point to Jesus. In fact, the whole sacrificial system pointed to the ultimate sacrifice Jesus would offer for us.

And why did Jesus have to actually shed his blood as a sacrifice for humanity? Let's see how the writer of Hebrews relates Jesus to the Mosaic law.

"When every commandment had been told to all the people by Moses in accordance with the law, he took the blood of calves and goats, with water and scarlet wool and hyssop, and sprinkled both the scroll itself and all the people, saying, 'This is the blood of the covenant that God has ordained for you.' And in the same way he sprinkled with the blood both the tent and all the vessels used in worship. Indeed, under the law almost everything is purified with blood, and without the shedding of blood there is no forgiveness of sins.

"Thus it was necessary for the sketches of the heavenly things to be purified with these rites, but the heavenly things themselves need better sacrifices than these. For Christ did not enter a sanctuary made by human hands, a mere copy of the true one, but he entered into heaven itself, now to appear in the presence of God on our behalf. Nor was it to offer himself again and again, as the high priest enters the Holy Place year after year with blood that is not his own; for then he would have had to suffer again and again since the foundation of the world. But as it is, he has appeared once for all at the end of the age to remove sin by the sacrifice of himself. And just as it is appointed for mortals to die once, and after that the judgment, so Christ, having been offered once to bear the sins of many, will appear a second time, not to deal with sin, but to save those who are eagerly waiting for him" (Hebrews 9:19–28).

Jesus himself said, "For this is my blood of the covenant, which is poured out for many for the forgiveness of sins" (Matthew 26:28).

In chapter 4, Hebrews relates another important Old Testament institution to Jesus. According to the writer of Hebrews, the Sabbath not only honors God's day off after six days of creation but is also a picture of the rest our souls find in Jesus and of the eternal rest we will find in heaven. "A sabbath rest still remains for the people of God; for those who enter God's rest also cease from their labors as God did from his" (Hebrews 4:9–10).

In chapter 9, Hebrews compares the Old Testament tabernacle and temple to the heavenly sanctuary in which Jesus serves as our high priest. "For Christ did not enter a sanctuary made by human hands, a mere copy of the true one, but he entered into heaven itself, now to appear in the presence of God on our behalf" (Hebrews 9:24).

∞∞∞∞∞

Hebrews compares the Old Testament tabernacle and temple to the heavenly sanctuary, in which Jesus serves as our high priest.

∞∞∞∞∞

And in the great "Faith Chapter," Hebrews 11, the author discussed Old Testament figures who acted in faith, because they had a keen awareness of their heavenly destiny. Noah built an ark without seeing a drop of rain. Abraham left his home for a nomadic life because "he looked forward to the city that has foundations, whose architect and builder is God" (Hebrews 11:10). Moses sprinkled the blood at Passover to save the firstborn of Israel.

These heroes understood they were "strangers and foreigners on the earth." They glimpsed their promises "from a distance." They were "seeking a homeland," not an earthly home, but "a better country, that is, a heavenly one. Therefore God is not ashamed to be called their God; indeed, he has prepared a city for them" (Hebrews 11:13–14, 16).

The Wait of Glory

Impatience was a problem for the early Christians. Jesus had promised to return for them, and they were wondering *next week, next month?* As the years wore on, they saw more and more Christians dying, and they anticipated their own mortality.

Thus, the message of several New Testament epistles is *perseverance*. "Be patient, therefore, beloved, until the coming of the Lord," James said, adding, "Strengthen your hearts, for the coming of the Lord is near" (James 5:7–8).

Peter kept the promise in front of his readers, reminding them of their "inheritance that is imperishable, undefiled, and unfading, kept in heaven for you" (1 Peter 1:4). Awaiting their ultimate rescue, they can rejoice, "even if now for a little while you have had to suffer various trials, so that the genuineness of your faith . . . may be found to result in praise and glory and honor when Jesus Christ is revealed" (verses 6–7).

Revealed is a key word for Peter. The truth about Jesus and our salvation may be hidden now, but it will come to light at the end. It's all part of God's secret plan. "He [Jesus] was destined before the foundation of the world, but was revealed at the end of the ages for your sake" (verse 20).

❦❦❦❦❦

The truth about Jesus and our salvation may be hidden now, but it will come to light at the end. It's all part of God's secret plan.

❦❦❦❦❦

Other people won't get it, Peter acknowledged. They will doubt that God has any plan at all. "In the last days scoffers will come, scoffing and indulging their own lusts and saying, 'Where is the promise of his coming? For ever since our ancestors died, all things continue as they were from the beginning of creation!' . . . But do not ignore this one fact, beloved, that with the Lord one day is like a thousand years, and a thousand years are like one day. The Lord is not slow about his promise, as some think of slowness, but is patient with you, not wanting any to perish, but all to come to repentance" (2 Peter 3:3–4, 8–9).

Then Peter echoed the teachings of Jesus and Paul when he described the climactic transition. "But the

Does Revelation Really Predict the Future? Don't Some People Say Revelation Is About the Past and Present?

There are various theories about Revelation. Some people say most of it describes events that took place in the first century. The struggle between good and evil, they say, was going on between the church and the Roman Empire. Others try to track the events of history *since* the first century, finding parallels to the events in Revelation.

The ultimate vision of heaven is a glimpse into our future. John is told to write "what you have seen, what is, and what is to take place after this" (Revelation 1:19), and it's likely this book covers all those bases. So even if parts of it describe the past and present, it also shows us our future home.

day of the Lord will come like a thief, and then the heavens will pass away with a loud noise, and the elements will be dissolved with fire ... the heavens will be set ablaze and dissolved ... But, in accordance with his promise, we wait for new heavens and a new earth, where righteousness is at home" (verses 10, 12–13).

We find both terror and peace in these images of the end. The earth as we know it hurtles toward its final destruction, but we live holy and godly lives as our future destiny is revealed.

The apostle John reminds us: "Beloved, we are God's children now; what we will be has not yet been revealed. What we do know is this: when he is revealed, we will be like him, for we will see him as he is" (1 John 3:2). Jesus will be revealed as Lord, and ultimately it's always about nearness to our loving Lord.

The Revelation of Jesus Christ

Now we come to the last book of the Bible. It's not titled "Revelations," in the plural, as if it's a random collection of visions. Nor is it "The Revelation of St. John." It was revealed *to* John, not made up by him. It is "The Revelation of Jesus Christ," or just "Revelation."

We've just been reading in other New Testament epistles how Jesus will be revealed and how we will be revealed with him. That's the Revelation being talked about here. Jesus will be clearly displayed as the Lord of everything, as this world closes down and a new universe is born. Believers from every age will come out of their trials and be revealed as children of God, and we will see Jesus as he is, and we will be like him.

In Revelation, the Lord opens the curtain of heaven for a few minutes to let the beloved disciple see inside. "Now write what you have seen, what is, and what is to take place after this," Jesus told John (Revelation 1:19), and thankfully John has done so.

Don't miss the fact that Revelation is rooted in the down-to-earth experiences of the church. Seven

*In Revelation, the Lord opens the
curtain of heaven for a few minutes to let
the beloved disciple see inside.*

churches in Asia Minor (now Turkey) are addressed
specifically in the first three chapters. Each has its
strengths and weaknesses. Several of these churches
are struggling with persecution; some are fighting
heresy within their ranks; some are dealing with
complacency. Every one of them received a direct
message from Jesus: encouragement, challenge,
rebuke. He knows where they are; now he shows
them where he is.

Chapters 4 and 5 of Revelation invite us into a
heavenly worship service. Maybe you already attend
a really great church, but this is like nothing you've
ever seen. There is God's throne, glittering like
jewels, surrounded with a rainbow, and 24 other
thrones for the white-robed elders, each with a

crown of gold. Lightning, thunder, seven torches, and in front of God's throne, a sea of glass.

Have you ever tried to describe some complex thing to a child? They don't have the capability to comprehend everything you've seen, so you struggle to use their language—ice cream cones, fire trucks, crayons, and building blocks. We get that sense when we read Revelation, except *we're* the children. John saw something beyond description, and he grabbed this motley collection of words to give us some idea. It's full of sound, light, color, and people. A rock concert, but more. A sci-fi film, but more. Independence Day fireworks, but more.

And then there are the four "living creatures" (or "beasts") who circle the throne singing praises. These creatures have faces of animals and humans, with many eyes and wings. (Some scholars suggest these are the "cherubim" mentioned elsewhere in Scripture.) "Holy, holy, holy," they sing, and then the elders intone their homage: "You are worthy, our

Lord and God, to receive glory and honor and power, for you created all things, and by your will they existed and were created" (Revelation 4:11).

The question arises in Chapter 5: *Who is worthy to open the scroll?* The scroll is the future. And apparently it's not just a question of revealing the future but bringing it about. *Who will lead us into future redemption?*

The answer, of course, is Jesus—the Lion of Judah, Root of David, the Lamb that was slain. A hymn of praise is then launched toward him: "You are worthy to take the scroll and to open its seals, for you were slaughtered and by your blood you ransomed for God saints from every tribe and language and people and nation; you have made them to be a kingdom and priests serving our God, and they will reign on earth" (Revelation 5:9–10).

This is probably a picture of what has been going on in heaven—and what's happening right now. The Hebrew tone of the worship service suggests that the worshippers are Old Testament faithful, bowing at God's throne, while looking for a Redeemer. Then Jesus is revealed as the fulfillment of prophecy, the sacrificial Lamb who takes away the sin of the world. Because of his sacrifice, he is worthy to lead the story forward, to bring history to its exciting conclusion.

∽∽∽

Heaven is a dimension in which the cosmos is bathed in holiness.

Arthur O. Roberts
"Finding Heaven," *Christianity Today*

And then we're off on an adventure of seals broken, trumpets sounded, and bowls outpoured! Any bookstore these days will have a dozen volumes claiming to give you the precise interpretation of these chapters, exactly what will happen and when. Some people get carried away with this stuff, quarreling over every last syllable. It is worth your careful, reasoned study, however, and you might find a system that helps you understand these images. But don't get so deep into the details that you miss the main point: *God wins.*

We hate to ruin the ending for you, but that is the theme of this whole book. All you Christians suffering in Asia Minor or Siberia or Sudan, take heart! God wins! The forces of evil will put up a struggle, but Jesus will emerge victorious!

That drops us into our next heavenly event, the victory party in chapter 19. A great multitude in heaven sings, "Hallelujah!" They praise God for finally bringing judgment upon evil. The elders and creatures from our earlier scene now join in this Hallelujah chorus. "Let us rejoice and exult and give him the glory, for the marriage of the Lamb has come, and his bride has made herself ready" (Revelation 19:7).

Suddenly the victory party becomes a kind of bridal shower. Who are the happy couple? Well, the groom is identified as the Lamb—that's Jesus. And throughout Scripture, the bride of Christ is the church, his redeemed people. In Jewish tradition of that time, the bride waited with the bridal party while the groom traveled with his own entourage to meet her. What a great picture of Jesus' return! The church has been waiting for his arrival, and now he's finally here.

We'll see the wedding photos soon enough, but meanwhile there are some final skirmishes. At the end of chapter 20, we come to Judgment. This is the

My Father's house on high,
Home of my soul, how near
At times to faith's foreseeing eye
Thy golden gates appear!
Ah! then my spirit faints
To reach the land I love,
The bright inheritance of saints,
Jerusalem above.

James Montgomery,
"Forever with the Lord"

end of the world as we know it. "Then I saw a great white throne and the one who sat on it; the earth and the heaven fled from his presence, and no place was found for them" (Revelation 20:11). From this throne God judges all those who have died. (More about this judgment in the next chapter.)

New Heaven and Earth

*A*fter that historic judgment, John saw a New Heaven and a New Earth. "I saw the holy city, the New Jerusalem, coming down out of heaven from God, prepared as a bride adorned for her husband" (Revelation 21:2). As always, Jerusalem is the intersection of God and humanity. Here we see it graphically: this giant cube of a city suspended between heaven and earth. John heard a voice from the throne: "See, the home of God is among mortals. He will dwell with them; they will be his peoples, and God himself will be with them" (verse 3).

But wait! Didn't we say the bride of Christ was the church? Here we see the bride is the New Jerusalem. An angel tells John, "Come, I will show you the bride, the wife of the Lamb," and then shows John "the holy city Jerusalem coming down out of heaven from God" (verses 9–10). This is not a conflict of Scripture. What is the church? The collection of people who worship God through Jesus Christ. Jerusalem was always the center of worship for God's chosen people. Now the New Jerusalem welcomes those of every nation into the Christ-centered worship of God. It's not a discrepancy, but it makes a key point. Despite the elaborate description of this glorious city, the most important thing about it is the people who are there: God and those who worship God.

Virtually everything we're told about this city stems from the presence of God and his relationship with these worshippers.

❖ The God of Joy "will wipe every tear from their eyes ... mourning and crying and pain will be no more" (verse 4).

❖ Since he is the Author of Life, "Death will be no more" (verse 4).

❖ The glory of God makes the place shine "like a very rare jewel, like jasper, clear as crystal" (verse 11).

❖ The strength of God gives it "a great, high wall" (verse 12).

❖ The twelve gates honor his relationship with "the twelve tribes of the Israelites" (verse 12).

❖ The twelve foundations honor "the twelve apostles of the Lamb"(verse 14).

❖ Surprisingly, there's no temple in this Jerusalem "for its temple is the Lord God the Almighty and the Lamb" (verse 22).

❖ Neither sun nor moon is necessary "for the glory of God is its light, and its lamp is the Lamb" (verse 23).

And yes, John described pearl gates and streets of gold, surely a testament to God's glory and purity (verse 21). In addition, a river flows from the throne of God with "the water of life, bright as crystal" (Revelation 22:1). And there, beside the river, is the "tree of life" (verse 2), which bears a different kind of fruit each month.

That sounds familiar. The Garden of Eden had a river flowing through it, as well as "the tree of life" (Genesis 2:9). In fact, one of the reasons that Adam and Eve were expelled from the Garden of Eden after disobeying God was to keep them from eating the fruit of the tree of life. But now, in this eternal paradise, the fruit of that tree is free for the taking. The curse has been removed.

Our finite minds are ill-equipped to take in the full view. As Paul once said, quoting from Isaiah, "No eye has seen, no ear has heard, nor the human heart conceived, what God has prepared for those who love him" (1 Corinthians 2:9; see Isaiah 64:4).

Certainly the Lord's complete plans might be too awesome for us to understand, but don't miss the line Paul tacked on to Isaiah's prophecy: *"God has revealed it to us through the Spirit"* (verse 10). God lets us know what he wants us to know. The Spirit revealed this glimpse of our future heavenly home to John, and John has shared this revelation with us.

Lord,

I long for this day, spending eternity with you in this New Jerusalem. It sounds like an amazing place, but the best thing is that I'll be with you.

In Jesus' name. Amen.

Have a Nice Forever

What Will We Do All Day, Every Day?

So what will that heavenly existence be like? Will it get boring? Certainly not. The Bible spells out some of the activities that will fill our eternal days, and we can guess at others. When we start thinking outside of our three-dimensional, time-bound world, the possibilities are endless. God is the fullness that fills everything, and he will definitely fill our lives with good things.

Kids are funny. Come June, they're counting the milliseconds until school's out for the summer. "Just think, we'll be free. No more teachers, no more books. We can do anything we want, all day, every day." And the first day off, they play like crazy, exulting in their newfound freedom. But about halfway through the second week of summer vacation they're sitting glumly, bemoaning their tedium.

"We're really bored," they whine. "There's nothing left to do."

Unfortunately, some folks are afraid heaven will be like that. Oh, it will be nice to be free from our earthly stress and strife. We can tour the streets of gold and look at the mansions Jesus promised. And we might enjoy reunions with loved ones. Seeing Jesus and singing with the angels—that will be grand. For a day or two. As long as it's not *all* day.

But then what? What will we do there? What could possibly fill up our datebooks for all eternity?

Don't worry. There will be plenty for us to do. The Bible specifically describes some activities, and we can guess at others.

Singing

Music has a huge place in heaven. Several times in the Book of Revelation (5:11;

19:1) we find the "multitude" joining in to sing God's praise. That's us, folks. Singing has always been part of the earthbound worship of God. The Israelites sang at the banks of the Red Sea (Exodus 15), and Paul urged Christians: "With gratitude in your hearts sing psalms, hymns, and spiritual songs to God" (Colossians 3:16). We even have a songbook in the center of the Bible—the Book of Psalms. Why wouldn't there be singing in heaven?

Are you worried because you can't sing? Not even in the shower? Or maybe you simply don't like to sing.

Be this the eternal song
Through all the ages long
May Jesus Christ be praised.

Edward Caswall

Some people love to sing; others don't. So why is singing such an important part of heaven? Let's think about this for a moment.

Singing is like talking, only better. It's communication in a different dimension. The words you sing can carry a message, but the music carries your heart. Indeed, few activities are as powerful both mentally and emotionally.

When you do sing with others, there is the possibility for harmony, working with others to create a beautiful result. Sometimes it's singing the same melody and rhythm, and sometimes it's singing in harmony or counterpoint—all focused on a unified sound.

You work with others to create a beautiful result . . . Isn't this an image of the church's love in action?

Making Music

W̶hat about harps in heaven? Yes, they are specifically mentioned (Revelation 5:8). But throughout the ages, the worship of God has also been accompanied with a wide range of instruments. The last psalm calls for what sounds like a huge jazz band to fill not only the sanctuary but also the heavens.

Praise him with trumpet sound;

praise him with lute and harp!

Praise him with tambourine and dance;

praise him with strings and pipe!

Praise him with clanging cymbals;

praise him with loud clashing cymbals!

(Psalm 150:3–5)

As a person with very little musical ability, I always felt anxious about this. My pastor used to call upon us to join the choir with our "ten string instruments." That was his way of encouraging us to clap along. Maybe that's what I'll be doing in heaven.

Resting

In the middle of his heavenly vision, the apostle John is commanded to write, "Blessed are the dead who from now on die in the Lord." And the Spirit adds, "Yes . . . they will rest from their labors, for their deeds will follow them" (Revelation 14:13). Faithful believers have done their work; now it's time to relax.

Heaven is sort of the eternal Sabbath day. But keep in mind that Sabbath is not a time for mere inactivity. It is a time for restoration, for fun, for re-energizing.

∽◯∽◯∽

Oh, what the joy and the glory must be
Those endless Sabbaths the blessed ones see
Crown for the valiant, to weary ones rest
God shall be All, and in all ever blest.

Peter Abelard

For some Type A personalities, this may be exactly what they *don't* want. They're worried about eternal downtime when they love to be up and moving. Having a full schedule is the ultimate goal. But if you've just been up all night every night with a crying baby, or if you just spent all week cramming for college exams until the wee hours, or if you're still getting used to that construction job, or if your new teaching position requires you to set your alarm for 4 A.M., or if your aging body just can't handle the activity you're used to—then rest might be very welcome.

God rested after six days of work, and he designed us to do the same. Heaven is sort of the eternal Sabbath day. But keep in mind that Sabbath is not a time for mere inactivity. It is a time for restoration, for fun, for re-energizing.

Students at a conservative Christian college successfully protested a policy of locking the tennis courts on Sunday. "Close the library if you want to keep us from studying on the Lord's Day," they argued, "but please give us a chance for recreation."

Maybe what that means is that we will ... be open to the joy we had when we were in our youth.

Enjoying

*A*nd as long as we're talking about recreation, isn't it *re-creation*—that is, creating ourselves anew? One prophet's vision of the New Jerusalem included this tidbit: "And the streets of the city shall be full of boys and girls playing in its streets" (Zechariah 8:5). What does that mean to those of us who stopped playing in the streets a very long time ago? Maybe what that means is that we will be re-creating and thus be open to the joy we had when we were in our youth.

Serving

In case you think you'll have nothing productive to do in heaven, there are indications that we will be actively "serving" God. In Scripture, the word for service is closely connected to the word for worship. This comes from the fact that there were many tasks involved in preparing the tabernacle (and later the Temple) for worship. Lamps needed trimming; altars needed cleaning; incense had to be placed on the coals. Without a temple, heaven won't have the same requirements. But we will worship and serve the Lord (see Reve-lation 7:15; 22:3). Who knows what sort of duties God will have for us? Surely we will be glad to do them.

Ruling

The details of this responsibility are unclear, but the Bible says we will be rulers with Christ, judging the new world order on his behalf. "Do you not know that the saints will judge the world?" Paul said. "Do you not know that we are to judge angels?" (1 Corinthians 6:2–3). In Revelation we see certain believers on thrones, "given authority to judge" (Revelation 20:4). Even the crowns we receive as rewards may be an indication of our authority as subrulers.

Adam and Eve were given "dominion" over the earth at its beginning (Genesis 1:28). That didn't work out too well. But God will redeem the earth as he has redeemed humanity.

The Banquets

We look forward to feasting with our family and friends. It is a special occasion that is often described in the Bible. In particular in the closing chapters of Revelation, we are invited to the marriage supper of the Lamb. When Jesus told his parables about the kingdom of heaven, he often set them at banquets or parties. That tells us something about Jesus. It also tells us something about heaven.

And, of course, we'll find many party-related activities there. Truly, *rejoicing* will be frequent in heaven. Jesus mentioned the angels' joy when the lost are found (Luke 15:7, 10), and Jude concluded his epistle with a benediction to the one "who is able

... to make you stand without blemish in the presence of his glory with rejoicing (Jude 24).

⋙⋙⋙

What's more, those relationships will be redeemed...
and centered on our mutual devotion to the Lord.

⋙⋙⋙

Eating and drinking will go on, or at least some heavenly equivalent. We know from Scripture that Jesus ate breakfast with his disciples after his resurrection (see John 21:12), so our resurrected bodies should have that same ability, if not the same need. Besides, it's difficult to "feast" without food. Jesus explicitly said, "Many will come from east and west and will eat with Abraham and Isaac and Jacob in the kingdom of heaven" (Matthew 8:11).

What's more, those relationships will be redeemed, of course, and centered on our mutual devotion to the Lord, but why wouldn't we share a great time with our family and friends?

*We will be seeing Christ in all his glory
and seeing ourselves for who we really
are—the ones he has made us to be.*

The End Without End

No doubt we haven't even dreamed of other heavenly activities. To assume that we'd grow weary of singing or resting or feasting would be extremely nearsighted. Heaven will be an endless stream of newness, as well as of love, life, and learning.

As St. Augustine came to the end of his epic work *City of God*, he pondered this very question of what we'll do in heaven. He put it poetically:

We shall rest and we shall see;

We shall see and we shall love;

We shall love and we shall praise.

See, this will be in the end without end.

For what is our end

But to reach the kingdom that won't end?

We will be seeing Christ in all his glory and seeing ourselves for who we really are—the ones he has made us to be. We will love him more fully than ever. All the while, we will be finding new and exciting ways to praise the King of Kings and Lord of Lords.

Lord,
I trust you to make heaven fulfilling and enjoyable. I'm not sure of all the activities you have planned for us, but I know you will be there, and I'm looking forward to that.

In Jesus' name. Amen.

Getting There

How to Ensure a Heavenly Future

What does the Bible say about getting to heaven? Contrary to popular opinion, our good deeds don't get us there. Only God's grace can do that. We receive his free gift of eternal life, and then he helps us live righteous lives.

It was one of those survival camps where they take a bunch of teenagers into the forest to learn self-esteem and other life lessons. Throughout the week, Sherry was highly motivated to prove herself. She ran faster, carried more, and navigated through the woods better than most of the campers on the trip.

On the last day, many of the different challenges of the week were gathered together in one "final exam" of sorts. Sherry set her sights on getting the highest score and beating her nemesis, Brandon. She was well on her way to that goal when she had to confront the Monster Wall. It was like rock-climbing, except it was a 20-foot wall with hand-holds cut at odd intervals. It would take both strength and smarts to scale.

Can I Know I'm Going to Heaven for Sure?

We receive God's gift through faith. The Bible describes faith as "the assurance of things hoped for, the conviction of things not seen" (Hebrews 11:1). You might call faith heart-knowledge. We rest on the promises of God, which have proven true time and time again.

Is that "knowing for sure"? Yes, in a heart-sense. The Bible uses the language of knowing. Paul talked about knowing Christ (Philippians 3:10) and knowing the love of Christ (Ephesians 3:19), as well as knowing the truth about God (2 Timothy 2:25). So knowing is not just a mental acceptance but a whole-person involvement.

In that sense, we can know God with our whole heart and then trust that what he said about our eternal destiny is true.

Sherry watched as several others failed to get even halfway up. A few, like Brandon, made it most of the way but had to be helped over by the group leader, Tim, who was positioned at the top of the platform. Then it was Sherry's turn. Taking a novel approach, she zigzagged her way up the wall, finding the handholds that would help her. She was just a few feet from the top when she got stymied. There was no way for her to get any higher. She scrambled down a bit then climbed at another angle. Still, she couldn't reach the top.

"Come on, Sherry," Tim called to her while extending his hand. "I've got you."

"No," she replied. "I can do this."

"You've done great, Sher. Just take my hand."

She refused.

"I've helped others; I can help you," Tim urged. "It's not a problem."

"No way," Sherry grunted. "I can beat this Monster Wall."

But she couldn't. After several approaches, more pleading from Tim, and more refusals from Sherry, the allotted time was up.

At the campfire that night, each student got his or her scores from the final activities. Sherry had done quite well in many events, but she didn't get the highest score.

"Brandon got ahead on the Monster Wall," Tim explained.

"But you helped him over!" Sherry protested.

Tim smiled sympathetically. "I know. And I wish you had let me help you. I had to fail you on that event."

His love is not based on my performance. I haven't earned it; therefore, I can't lose it.

Brennan Manning, *The Signature of Jesus*

That seemed very wrong to her. "But I had to do it myself!" she insisted.

"Why?" the leader asked. "We never said that. A lot of times survival means knowing when to ask for help."

It was a hard lesson for Sherry to learn, but a good one. There's only so much you can do on your own.

Two Roads

After all this talk about heaven, the question might arise: *How do we get there?* The answer might seem simple to you, but biblically speaking, a lot of people get it wrong. There are actually two roads to heaven, and in the Bible you can find roadmaps for both of them. The problem is, only one of them works.

It's a matter of common sense, isn't it? Good people go to heaven! Everyone knows that. Your deeds are listed on some heavenly ledger, and if the good outweighs the bad, you're in. Right? Doesn't the Bible say that?

The answer might seem simple ...
but a lot of people get it wrong.

Well, yes it does. Sort of. But there's a catch.

You see, we're like the kids in Sherry's survival group. No one can get over that wall. Some of us are so bad we can climb only a few feet to heaven, and others are more like Sherry, grabbing one good deed after another, thinking they're going to make it. But no, there is really no way to climb into heaven on our own power.

"All have sinned and fall short of the glory of God," the Bible states (Romans 3:23), and elsewhere, "There is no one who is righteous, not even one" (verse 10). You can try to obey the Ten Commandments. You can try to follow every command of God. But you cannot be good enough for God. The Bible flatly states, "No one will be justified by the works of the law" (Galatians 2:16).

If you have questions about this, read through the Book of Romans, especially chapters 1—8, and follow the careful reasoning of the apostle Paul. *How can we get the righteousness that God requires?* That's the question Paul was posing. Our sin, he said, is a huge problem. It alienates us from God. You might be hoping that God will open the heavenly ledger someday and see that your charitable giving makes up for your lust or pride, but it won't work like that. We tend to think of our sinfulness as a traffic ticket or maybe a shoplifting rap that might easily be plea-bargained. God sees it more like murder. "The wages of sin is death," Paul explained, "but the free gift of God is eternal life in Christ Jesus our Lord" (Romans 6:23).

Any sin separates us from God. We cannot pay for our sins with our own good deeds. It takes a

God-size sacrifice, and—good news!—that's exactly what God offers. It's a free gift, and all we have to do is receive it. Like Tim, the group leader, he reaches out his hand to us. Will we let him lift us into heaven? That's the only way we're going to get there.

✧✧✧✧✧

It might be common sense to think that good deeds can win you a trip to heaven, but the New Testament says otherwise.

✧✧✧✧✧

"For by grace you have been saved through faith," Paul said in another letter, "and this is not your own doing; it is the gift of God—not the result of works, so that no one may boast" (Ephesians 2:8–9). It might be common sense to think that good deeds can win you a trip to heaven, but the clear message of the New Testament says otherwise. Oh, God loves it when we do good things, and he will help us do them, but the only way to reach heaven is to admit that you can't.

Final Judgment

Toward the end of the Book of Revelation, the apostle John described the passing of the old earth, at which is a scene of ultimate judgment. "Then I saw a great white throne and the one who sat on it; the earth and the heaven fled from his presence, and no place was found for them" (Revelation 20:11). The dead are brought before God and judged "according to their works." Books that have recorded all their deeds are opened, and the dead are judged.

Wait! What about salvation by grace? Was John saying we are ultimately judged by our works?

It sounds that way, but a crucial detail in this scene changes. "Another book was opened, the book of life" (verse 12). Ultimately, "anyone whose name was not found written in the book of life was thrown into the lake of fire" (verse 15).

We always have a choice. We may receive the grace of God or we may not. If we do, the blood of Christ becomes our payment for our sins, and our names are written in the book of life. If we refuse God's grace, we are, in effect, deciding to try to reach heaven on our own. It's a gutsy move but quite foolish, because no one can be good enough for God. The people who make this choice are "the dead" who are judged by their works. When those ledger books are opened, it is obvious that these people fall short of God's glorious perfection. Their sin has earned them the death penalty, and no amount of good behavior can change that. Without a Savior, they are doomed.

You don't hear a lot about hell these days, and we haven't said much about it in this book, but Scripture portrays it as a terrifying reality. It is usually described as a lake of fire, a place of enduring torment for those who reject the grace of God.

Sometimes people wonder, "How can a loving God send people to hell?" It's a good question, but when you consider his "free gift" of eternal life, the whole premise changes. God is doing all he can to bring people into heaven, short of making the decision for them. He freely offers salvation through Jesus, but he lets people choose whether to accept it or not.

The Narrow Gate

Jesus talked about two roads that lead beyond this earthly existence. "The gate is wide and the road is easy that leads to destruction, and there are many who take it" (Matthew 7:13). You might think he was talking about the way of sin, which far too many seem to be traveling. But in the context of his Sermon on the Mount, it's more likely that he's

❦

Praise, my soul, the King of heaven.
To the throne thy tribute bring.
Ransomed, healed, restored, forgiven,
Evermore God's praises sing:
Alleluia! Alleluia!
Praise the everlasting King.
Angels in the heights, adoring,
You behold God face to face.
Saints triumphant, now adoring,
Gathered in from every race.
Alleluia! Alleluia!
Praise with us the God of grace.

Henry F. Lyte

talking about self-righteousness—the determination to make it to heaven on your own merits. "Throw open those record books, and I'll bet my good deeds far outweigh my sins!" That's the road to destruction.

According to Jesus, however, the way of grace is the "narrow gate" and the "hard road." It's not easy to humble yourself, admit your sin, and grab his outstretched hand to pull you over. But that's the way "that leads to life, and there are few who find it" (Matthew 7:14).

So, how do you do this? How do you get to heaven? Jesus had said it simply a few verses earlier:

"Ask, and it will be given you; search, and you will find; knock, and the door will be opened for you. For everyone who asks receives, and everyone who searches finds, and for everyone who knocks, the door will be opened" (verses 7–8).

Lord,
I thank you for your free gift of eternal life.
Too often I try to get to heaven on my own
steam. I need your forgiveness. I need your
grace. I receive your gift.

In Jesus' name. Amen.

Eyes on the Prize

Living the Heavenly Minded Life

How does the hope of heaven affect your life on earth? It might give you joy in hard times. It might give you empathy for others. It might inspire you to deepen your relationship with God right now, even before you get to heaven.

He only had to get from the driveway to the door, but he was struggling with grocery bags. She was out on her power walk, and she rushed to help him, grabbing a bag before it dropped to the sidewalk.

"Thank you, thank you," he gushed. "That could have been a big mess."

"No problem," she replied as she placed the bag gently on the porch. "You sure you're all right?"

He nodded, and then asked, "Do you go to that church around the corner?"

"No," she smiled. "I don't."

"You should," the man said. "They've got a lot of people like you. Always helping folks. I think you'd fit right in."

That's the way it should work. Christians should be known for helping people, for loving people, and for being ready to meet needs. Why? Because we are connected to heaven. We are Heaven People. Ideally, our selfish desires are set aside because we're storing our treasure in heaven. We want to invest our time, energy, and resources in the securities that God recommends, among which is helping the needy.

We needn't be anxious about the bad news of this world, because our hope is in the good news of the world to come. We know our destination—we have received the gift of eternal life. But that life begins the moment we accept the gift.

Consider Olympic athletes. They shape their lives around one goal: winning the gold in the Olympic Games. That might be four long years away, but those athletes are singularly focused. Every aspect of their lives, every decision they make, brings them closer to their objective. That's the analogy Paul used when he wrote: "This one thing I do: forgetting what lies behind and straining forward to what lies ahead, I press on toward the goal for the prize of the heavenly call of God in Christ Jesus" (Philippians 3:13–14). Thinking of the Olympic athletes of his day, Paul urged Christians to have the same single-minded dedication to the goal of knowing Christ and living in the power of his resurrection.

Therefore, Christians can go through life leaning forward. We're going somewhere. We're not anchored to the temporary rewards of this world, because we know our riches are in the future.

Here's something to ponder. We normally think of *eternal* as an adjective about duration. Eternal life is life that goes on forever. But read what Jesus said about it: "This is eternal life," Jesus said in his majestic prayer concerning God and himself, "that they may know you, the only true God, and Jesus

Christ whom you have sent" (John 17:3). "Eternal life" takes on the quality of life. It is not just a matter of living a long time; it is being energized forever with the intimate knowledge of God and Christ.

So what does the heavenly kind of life look like here on earth? We could discuss many aspects of heaven, but let's pick six, conveniently spelling out H-E-A-V-E-N.

Humility

How do we get to heaven? By God's grace, not by our own efforts. If we think we're getting there by being good, then maybe we could boast a little and scorn those who didn't measure up to our level of righteousness. But we know that eternal life is a gift from God. We haven't earned it.

Jesus told a story about two men, a religious leader and a known sinner, who went to the Temple to pray. The leader proudly listed his accomplishments before the Lord. The other merely said, "God, be merciful to me, a sinner!" (Luke 18:13). Jesus shocked his listeners by announcing that the sinner, and not the religious leader, left that place justified before God (see verses 9–14).

In conversation, we may be shy about taking credit—but still look down on other people. That's not what Christian humility is about. Boasting is not just bad form, it's bad thinking. True humility is not a matter of *seeming* humble, but of realizing that we have nothing to boast about. As Christians we are not better than anyone else. We are just recipients of grace.

Empathy

"By this everyone will know that you are my disciples, if you have love for one another" (John 13:35). With those words, Jesus set the bar for his followers. To be a Christian is to love and to be perceived as loving. Faith and hope are great, enduring qualities, Paul wrote, but "the greatest of these is love" (1 Corinthians 13:13). When asked to name the greatest commandment, Jesus again spoke of love—loving God with everything we've got and loving our neighbors as ourselves.

That's fascinating phraseology. But how do we love our neighbor *as ourself* when doing so goes against our tendency to put ourself first? When we love others the way Jesus wants, we then have the same motivation to care for them. Their needs become ours. Their burdens are on our backs. This kind of love prepares us for heaven.

<hr />

*True humility is not a matter of seeming
humble, but of realizing that we have
nothing to boast about.*

Adoration

〜

*M*ost of us can probably recall a bad case of puppy love. Nowadays a teenage guy might make a photo of his new girlfriend the screen saver on his computer. He can stare at her whenever he wants. What's he doing? He's adoring her.

One thing about adoration: It doesn't seem very practical. A parent might advise a lovesick teen to quit swooning and do something useful.

Some people in our churches might say something similar. "Why is all this time spent in worship when we could be doing something that makes a difference?" Don't listen to those folks. According to reports in Revelation, we'll be spending a substantial part of eternity in worshipful adoration of our Lord. Why not get started now? Keep gazing into the Lord's face, think about him often, tell him how great he is, and tell others as frequently as possible.

Victory

～

*R*emember the main theme of Revelation? *God wins!* In our ongoing struggle with sin and sorrow, it's good to know we're on the winning team. It's Friday, but Sunday's coming!

Some Christians worry a lot. They fret about to where the nation's heading. They're upset about terrorism. To them the local government is packed with incompetent officials, and the schools are teaching falsehoods. It's one thing after another. What's this world coming to?

Well, the world is coming to an end, and then God will make everything new. That's the assurance we have as Christians. There is struggle, but there is

∽∾∽

The love of heaven makes one heavenly.

William Shakespeare

also victory. We are assured that life will be difficult. "But take courage," Jesus said. "I have conquered the world!" (John 16:33).

Enjoyment

〰️

As Christians we have God inside us, and so we can greet each day with joy. Indeed, the Bible erupts with joy. "Rejoice in the Lord always; again I will say, Rejoice" (Philippians 4:4). Joy is listed as number two on the chart of the fruit the Spirit produces in our lives (Galatians 5:22).

Amazingly, much of the Bible's discussion of joy also includes adversity. "My brothers and sisters, whenever you face trials of any kind, consider it nothing but joy" (James 1:2). James was picking up on a theme from Jesus: "Blessed are you when people revile you and persecute you and utter all kinds of evil against you falsely on my account. Rejoice

and be glad, for your reward is great in heaven"
(Matthew 5:11–12).

Our heavenly future allows us to put our earthly
struggles in perspective. As the psalmist said, "Weeping may linger for the night, but joy comes with the
morning" (Psalm 30:5). And whatever difficulties we
may be facing now, we look with joy toward the
Son-rise that will change everything.

So hard times are no excuse for moping. Oh, sure,
there's a time to weep. Christian joy doesn't ignore
the sorrows of life. But with God inside us, we can
be assured that our future home is full of joy.

Nearness

O f all the many things we've learned about
heaven on these pages, the most important
is this: Heaven is where God is. Golden streets and
pearly gates will be glorious to behold, but the most

important thing about heaven is God's presence. We will be with him.

And so, even now, as we prepare for the heavenly part of our eternal life, we can practice nearness to God by entwining him in our lives. He's *around* us all the time, but do we really invite him into the daily grind?

Do you say good morning to God when you get up? Some take time for prayer and Bible reading every morning, and that's a wonderful habit to get into. But others don't really wake up until noon. That's fine, but could you at least say "hi" to God?

Do you bring your daily needs and worries to God? When you face a challenge in your work, do you ask him for help? Do you thank him when he provides it? Paul wrote, "Do not worry about anything, but in everything ... with thanksgiving let your requests be made known to God" (Philippians 4:6).

Is the Lord a part of your relationships? Is he woven into your marriage? Do you talk about him with your spouse, your kids, or your parents? Family devotional time is great idea, but don't force God to stay in that corner. Welcome him into your home at many times.

After writing about Jesus' return, Paul gave the Thessalonians some quick-fire advice: "Rejoice always, pray without ceasing, give thanks in all circumstances" (1 Thessalonians 5:16–18). Always? Without ceasing? Isn't the apostle exaggerating a bit?

Not necessarily. Our heavenly existence will be a nonstop nearness to the Lord we love. Why can't that start now?

Lord,
Come and be a part of my life—always,
without ceasing, in all circumstances. I want
to start living my eternal life right now.
In Jesus' name. Amen.